RAISING A JIHADI GENERATION
Understanding the Muslim Brotherhood Movement in America

**A Handbook for Law Enforcement, Intelligence
and Military Professionals**

RAISING A JIHADI GENERATION

Understanding the Muslim Brotherhood Movement in America

By John Guandolo

ISBN 978-0-9887245-0-1

Printed in the USA

IN THEIR OWN WORDS

"According to the Islamic *shari'a* that Allah [has bequeathed] to mankind, the status of the Muslims, compared to that of the infidel nations that arrogantly [disdain] his *shari'a*, is measured in a kind of scale, in which one side is in a state of superiority, the other is in a state of inferiority..."

"[Arab and Muslim Regimes] are disregarding Allah's commandment to wage jihad for His sake with [their] money and [their] lives, so that Allah's word will reign supreme and the infidels' word will be inferior..."

"[Arab and Muslim Regimes] crucially need to understand that the improvement and change that the [Muslim] nation seeks can only be attained through jihad and sacrifice and by **raising a jihadi generation that pursues death just as the enemies pursue life**..."

"The U.S. is now experiencing the beginning of its end, and is heading towards its demise..."

"The Muslim nation has the means [to bring about] improvement and change...It knows the way, the methods, and the road signs, and it has a practical role model in Allah's Messenger, [the Prophet Muhammad]... who clarified how to implement the values of the [Koran] and the Sunna at every time and in every place."

- Mohammed Badie
Supreme Guide of the International Muslim Brotherhood
September 2010

This handbook is dedicated to all the brave men and women who serve on the streets of America and overseas so the rest of us can live free and secure.

ABOUT THE AUTHOR

John Guandolo is the Founder of UnderstandingTheThreat.com, an organization dedicated to providing strategic and operational threat-focused consultation, education, and training for federal, state and local leadership and agencies.

Mr. Guandolo is a 1989 graduate of the U.S. Naval Academy and took a commission as an Officer in the United States Marine Corps. He served with 2d Battalion 2d Marines as an Infantry Platoon Commander in combat Operations Desert Shield/Storm. From 1991-1996, he served in 2d Force Reconnaissance Company as a Platoon Commander, Assistant Operations Officer, and the unit's Airborne and Diving Officer. During this time, he also deployed to the Adriatic/Bosnia. He served for one year as the Unit Leader for the CINC's In-Extremis Force, directly reporting to a Combatant Commander in a classified mission profile. Mr. Guandolo was a combat diver, a military freefall parachutist, and is a graduate of the U.S. Army Ranger School.

In 1996, Mr. Guandolo resigned his commission in the Marine Corps and joined the Federal Bureau of Investigation (FBI), serving at the Washington Field Office. From 1996-2000, he primarily conducted narcotics investigations domestically and overseas. In 2001, he served for one year as the FBI Liaison to the U.S. Capitol Police investigating threats on the President, Vice-President, Members of Congress and other high-level government officials.

Shortly after 9/11, Mr. Guandolo began an assignment to the Counterterrorism Division of the FBI's Washington Field Office developing an expertise in the Muslim Brotherhood, Islamic Doctrine, the global Islamic Movement, and a myriad of terrorist organizations to include Hamas, Al Qaeda, and others. In 2006, Mr. Guandolo created and implemented the FBI's first Counterterrorism Training/Education Program focusing on the Muslim Brotherhood and their subversive movement in the United States, Islamic Doctrine, and the global Islamic Movement. He was designated a "Subject Matter Expert" by FBI Headquarters. This course was hailed as "groundbreaking" by the FBI's

Executive Assistant Director in a brief to the Vice President's National Security Staff. For his efforts, in 2007 Mr. Guandolo was presented the "Defender of the Homeland" Award by U.S. Senators John Kyl and Joseph Lieberman on behalf of the Center for Security Policy in Washington, D.C. While in the FBI, Mr. Guandolo received two United States Attorney's Awards for Investigative Excellence.

Mr. Guandolo served on the Washington Field Office SWAT team for over nine years and as its Team Leader for three of those years. He was a certified Undercover Agent, and served in a variety of assignments in that capacity. Mr. Guandolo was a Nationally Registered Paramedic, a First Aid Instructor, and served as an "Advanced Capability Medic" with the FBI. His career has included significant overseas travel to include many areas of Africa, Southwest Asia, Europe and elsewhere. In his last year and a half in the FBI, Mr. Guandolo served on a Surveillance Unit.

Mr. Guandolo advises governments - U.S. and others - on matters related to National Security, specifically the threat from the Global Islamic Movement. He actively advises members of Congress, law enforcement, the intelligence community, military, National Guard, key community leaders, and others. He served as an adjunct instructor at the Joint Forces Staff College and the U.S. Army War College, and is one of the authors of the "Shariah – The Threat to America," the first comprehensive book on the threat from the Islamic Movement in the U.S. He frequently appears on television and radio, and regularly publishes articles related to these matters in a number of media outlets.

AUTHOR'S NOTE

In June 2011, I, along with two colleagues, delivered a three-day program at the Headquarters Marine Corps auditorium (Arlington, Virginia) to approximately 115 law enforcement and national security professionals.

Represented were the major federal agencies – FBI, CIA, NSA, DIA, DHS, and others – as well as numerous law enforcement officers from the FBI Joint Terrorism Task Forces (JTTFs) across the Maryland, Virginia, and D.C. areas. Additionally, several individuals from Special Operations units were in attendance as well as members of the FBI's National Joint Terrorism Task Force.

The program was entitled *"Understanding the Threat to America"* and focused on: the Muslim Brotherhood's Movement in the United States including history, doctrine, structure, modus operandi, organizations, leadership, and penetration into our system; Shariah (Islamic Law), specifically as it is used by our enemies to wage Jihad against us; and, finally, why this information is important to local and state police officers, military personnel, and federal agencies, and what can be done about this threat.

Before lunch on the third day, a gentleman stood up and, in front of over 100 of his colleagues said, "John, I have been in the FBI for over fourteen years. I am a supervisor at FBI Headquarters in the Counterterrorism Division, and I have never heard any of the information you all have put out here." He went on and explained how angry he was and used some very colorful language to relate that anger to us that day. He did say, however, we had demonstrated the information we presented was true without question, as we used facts and evidence.

I looked around the crowd and said, "Raise your hand if you knew this information before you came in here on Day 1?"

Can you guess how many hands went up? One would hope that with the FBI's National Joint Terrorism Task Force personnel, CIA, DHS, JTTF representatives, and others in the room, many hands would shoot up. So how many hands went up?

ZERO.

Well, to be honest, seven hands went up, but those were members of a local law enforcement agency who attended our same program a few months earlier in March 2011.

How is it possible that the very agencies charged with national security responsibilities know nothing of the Muslim Brotherhood's Movement in the U.S. or the doctrine that they – and Al Qaeda – specifically state is the reason for which they do what they do?

It is not random - that I can assure you. It is the intentional outcome of a decades-long Movement led by the Muslim Brotherhood in this country working to destroy our way of life and impose Shariah (Islamic Law) through the vehicle of Jihad.

For those who believe the Brotherhood's objectives are so far-fetched as to be unattainable, I would offer this: If a man walked up to you on the street, grabbed you by the scruff of the collar and said, "I have a gun in my pocket and I am going to pull it out and kill you," is it prudent to dismiss him by saying, "he doesn't mean it." Is it a sane response to say, "He doesn't know how to work a gun?" Or is the best response to assume he means it and act accordingly.

The Muslim Brotherhood has been in America for over 50 years. They have a written strategic plan and a plan to implement the strategy. They are well-funded, well-organized and have a network of thousands of organizations in America alone working daily to achieve their objectives.

The very organizations in the U.S. government charged with defending Americans against such a threat do not even know this threat exists. What do you think their chance of long-term success is?

The enemy in this war has convinced us to dismiss every jihadi who steps in front of us. The good men and women on the street are missing key parts of their training on the threat we face, thus putting them and the communities they seek to protect in danger.

I am hopeful this book will take great strides to close this gap so our brave men and women at the ground level can close with and crush the threat that is sitting on our doorstep.

John Guandolo
August 2013

TABLE OF CONTENTS

INTRODUCTION

This handbook is the first of its kind to examine the history, writings and practical implementation of the Muslim Brotherhood's strategic plan to overthrow the United States.

It focuses on tools for professionals in the law enforcement, intelligence, and military communities. It must be understood **that the Muslim Brotherhood in America prepares the ground for, supports, and facilitates jihadi operations.**

Once the information provided in this handbook is understood, it necessarily gives security and intelligence professionals a factual basis to address the enemy, changes what constitutes reasonable suspicion/probable cause, and transforms how this threat is approached and addressed.

As this Handbook makes clear, the Muslim Brotherhood has operatives in our federal law enforcement and intelligence agencies, our military, but, most importantly, advising our senior leadership in our national security apparatus.

This problem is much more a counterintelligence and espionage problem than it is a counterterrorism problem.

Once the control the Muslim Brotherhood has within the U.S. government's decision-making process is understood, it becomes clear America faces an insurgency inside our homeland, which requires a very different response, especially from local law enforcement.

In a counterinsurgency, the focus of the main effort is at the local level. Local police, working together with their local council, are the first line of defense against this enemy. But first you must have an educated and energized local populous.

It is our hope you will read and study what is contained herein. The information has been broken down in a usable form without losing the real depth of thought and effort by our adversary. This is an enemy who is cunning, patient, well-supported and well-organized.

To underestimate this enemy is to lose the war.

FOREWORD

As we learned in the 1990s, and are relearning today, there are significant downsides to making the civilian criminal justice our nation's preferred counterterrorism weapon. A foreign enemy force that projects force globally and on a massive scale is not a mere criminal defendant; to treat it as such is a provocative display of weakness that can only embolden those for whom killing Americans is a core objective.

All that said, however, the Justice Department's prosecution of terrorism cases has had one advantage unequaled by any other component of the government's counterterrorism arsenal: The common sense of juries.

Unlike politically correct agency press offices and ideological journalists, jurors are given the responsibility of deciding issues of immense importance because they are vetted for objectivity and bring to their deliberations the community's good judgment. They will not convict accused terrorists and their abettors absent a compelling demonstration of not only what was done but why it was done.

Consequently, the trials of Islamic supremacists – from the 1993 World Trade Center bombing, through such al Qaeda atrocities as the 1998 bombing of American embassies in Eastern Africa, to the Holy Land Foundation conspiracy to underwrite Hamas's intifada against Israel – developed a comprehensive and convincing exposition of the enemy's doctrine.

Grasping that doctrine is the bedrock of our national security, the only way we can know what motivates the enemy, how he operates, and what he is apt to do next. That is why *Raising a Jihadi Generation: Understanding the Muslim Brotherhood Movement in America* is such a desperately needed contribution.

The word "desperately" is not overwrought. For two decades, there has been a wayward campaign in the West to obscure the Islamic supremacist ideology. This seems absurd on its face: Putting aside the obvious wisdom in Sun Tzu's ancient epigram, "Know your enemy," what would the West look like today if the United States and its freedom-loving allies refused to examine and plan their national defenses around the totalitarian ideologies of Nazi Germany or the Soviet Union? Yet, our government's national security components – law enforcement, military, and intelligence – have steadfastly resisted undertaking what jurors, in their common sense, have always seen as a basic obligation of service: the need to know why.

John Guandolo, who has produced this invaluable primer, comes at the task from a unique perspective, having served as a Marine and an FBI Special Agent. *Raising a Jihadi Generation* is presented in a pamphlet form: It is succinct, extraordinarily well organized – with brief chapters and logical sub-headings – and fact-laden, which is to say: heavily reliant on what has been proved in court and what is undeniably written in the core texts revered by Islamic supremacists. It gets right to the heart of what a competent investigator or intelligence operative would need to know in order to do his or her job.

Necessarily, the main focus is on the Muslim Brotherhood, the most important and effective grass-roots movement in radical Islam. While the Brotherhood has methodological differences with groups like al Qaeda – seeing violent jihadism as just one essential item on a broad menu of tactics rather than its principal means of conquest – they are on the same ideological page.

The Brotherhood, founded in the 1920s, has been the most systematic of all Islamic supremacist organizations in terms of developing and preserving jihadist doctrine – including, of course, the catalyzing imperative of implementing sharia, Islam's societal framework and legal code. Its rigorous indoctrination program, internal discipline, and patience in building capacity have enabled its franchises to have powerful impact worldwide, and many of its members have gone on to found and contribute to other jihadist organizations. Thus, understanding how the enemy operates in our midst is impossible without understanding the Brotherhood.

Our agencies, like our opinion elites, have been derelict in this duty. In part, this is explained by political correctness and a well-meaning desire not to offend Muslims – a tragically counterproductive mindset since appeasement of the Brotherhood suppresses authentically moderate and pro-American Muslims.

In part, it is explained by the ascendancy in politics, media and academe of progressives, whose default position is that threats to American national security are natural responses to American arrogance, not rooted in a supremacist ideology that predates America by many centuries. And in part, it owes to the success of the enemy doctrine itself, which prizes infiltration of a target society's opinion-driving institutions.

Raising a Jihadi Generation is a badly needed corrective to this dereliction. A law enforcement agent, an intelligence officer, or a military adviser who spent an hour reading it would learn more than any student of the government's trendy and extensive "Muslim outreach" courses, many of which are actually designed and vetted for approval by Brotherhood sympathizers.

More importantly, members of the government's national security agencies who read *Raising a Jihadi Generation*, and who are wise enough to keep it nearby as a handy reference, will be far better equipped to protect the United States.

That is, they will be performing their sworn duty.

Andrew C. McCarthy
Former Chief Assistant United States Attorney,
Southern District of New York
Senior Fellow, National Review Institute
Bestselling author, most recently, of
Spring Fever: The Illusion of Islamic Democracy

SECTION 1:

A BRIEF HISTORY OF THE MUSLIM BROTHERHOOD

After World War I and the Turkish Revolution, national hero Mustapha Kemal "Ataturk" ("Father of the Turks") became the founder and first President of Turkey.

In the early 1920's Ataturk attempted to abolish all Islamic influence in Turkey in favor of European influences and establish secular rule. Ataturk ended the nearly 700 year old Islamic Caliphate, known as the "Ottoman Empire," and banned the growing of beards by men and wearing of scarves by women. He also banned the call to prayer, abolished Arabic script and replaced it with Latin script, built a secular/western-styled legal system, and made the Turkish military the defenders of secular Turkey.

Dissolving the Islamic Caliphate and transforming Turkey from the center of the Islamic world to a secular nation did not sit well with the global Muslim community (Ummah). In 1928, the son of a prominent Imam outside of Cairo, Egypt named Hassan al Banna created the Society of Muslim Brothers or the Muslim Brotherhood *(al-Ikhwan al-Muslimin)*.

The Muslim Brotherhood (MB) was created to unify the Islamic states, expand the Caliphate, and subordinate all lands under the Caliphate to the Sharia (Islamic Law). Their By-Laws specifically state:

> **"The Muslim Brotherhood is an International Muslim Body, which seeks to establish Allah's law in the land."**

The MB goals are listed in their By-Laws as:

> **"Insist to liberate the Islamic nation from the yoke of foreign rule...the need to work on establishing the Islamic State...the sincere support for a global cooperation in accordance with the provisions of the Islamic Sharia."**

By the early 1930's, the Brotherhood formalized its organizational structure and formed groups of men with unique spiritual and physical training called "Battalions." By 1940, the Brotherhood created the Special Section, the military wing of the MB which conducts offensive operations such as ambushes, kidnappings, assassinations, etc.

During the 1940's and World War II, the Brotherhood pushed for Egyptian society to become increasingly adherent to Sharia (Islamic Law), and called for the removal of all British forces from Egypt.

During the late 1940's, the Brotherhood assassinated Egyptian officials and British soldiers and their families. In December of 1948, a Muslim Brother assassinated Egyptian Prime Minister Mahmud Fahmi al-Nuqrashi. In February 1949, the Egyptian security services gunned down Muslim Brotherhood founder Hassan al Banna in Cairo.

The time following the death of al Banna is marked with significant violence in Egypt against the government and the British. During this time, the Brotherhood's influence spread throughout the Middle East and into the West. It is estimated that by the time the Brotherhood came to the United States in the 1950's it had hundreds of branches in dozens of countries.

As you will see, when the Muslim Brotherhood came to America, it came with a plan. They call it the "Process of Settlement" which details how they insinuated themselves into our society, grew their numbers, strength and support, and began to work towards their objective of overthrowing the United States by "Civilization Jihad."

The very first national Islamic organization in the United States was the Muslim Students Association (MSA), formed in 1962 at the University of Illinois in Urbana – and it was created by the Muslim Brotherhood.

From the MSA nearly every major Islamic organization in North America was formed. Today there are over 600 MSA chapters at colleges and universities across America working to recruit members to the Muslim Brotherhood and to the jihad. There is likely an MSA chapter close by as you read this.

Right now, there are thousands of Muslim Brotherhood front organizations working across America to achieve their goals. As you go forward in this book ask yourself, "How is my organization vetting individuals and organizations to ensure they are not a part of this hostile and clearly dangerous movement in my community?"

SECTION 2:

STRUCTURE OF THE MUSLIM BROTHERHOOD

The Muslim Brotherhood has a presence in over 100 countries around the world. They are headquartered in Cairo, Egypt. Their official English website, www.Ikhwanweb.com is based in London, England. The following is a brief breakdown of their structure at the international and national levels.

The International Muslim Brotherhood

Chairman (Supreme Masul/Guide):

- The Movement's Overall Leader

- "He is expected to supervise the entire group's units, give advice, guidance and direct officials and hold them accountable for every fault, failure, corruption, deviation or disregard and neglect of rules according to the group's regulations." (MB By-Laws, Article 12, A)

Executive Guidance Bureau

- Made up of 14 Members

- "Brotherhood's senior executive and administrative board as well as watchdog authorized to conduct the policy-oriented management plans and mechanisms which would form the basis of the group." (MB By-Laws, Article 23)

General Shura Council

- The Shura Council is made up of at least 30 members from Shura Councils in countries around the world

- "The Shura Council is the Brotherhood's legislative authority and its decisions are binding." (MB By-Laws, Article 36)

- The "legislative authority" pertains to matters of Islamic Law (Sharia).

The Muslim Brotherhood in Nations Around the World

<u>**General Masul (Guide)**</u>

- Leader of the Muslim Brotherhood in that nation

Organizational Conference

- Executive and administrative board to direct policy and direction of the group

<u>**Shura Council**</u>

- Legislative authority for Muslim Brotherhood operations

- Ensures compliance with Sharia

In every country where the Brotherhood exists, they establish political organizations, social organizations, and their military wing or Special Section, which will be discussed further in Section 5 of this handbook.

SECTION 3:

MUSLIM BROTHERHOOD DOCTRINE

The following is a listing of key Muslim Brotherhood doctrine. It is clear, concise, and consistent.

MB Creed: "Allah is our goal; the Messenger is our guide: the Koran is our law; Jihad is our means; and martyrdom in the way of Allah is our inspiration."

MB Logo: The MB logo, seen below, has a green circular background signifying the world dominated by Islam, two crossed swords with a Koran above them with a single Arabic word underneath the swords. The word is "PREPARE" or "Make Ready" and, as the Muslim Brotherhood has publicly declared, is a direct reference to chapter 8, verse 60 of the Koran which states:

> "Against them make ready your strength to the utmost of your power, including steeds of war, to strike terror into the hearts of the enemies of Allah and your enemies..."

The following is taken verbatim from the Muslim Brotherhood By-Laws:

Chapter II: Objectives and means

Article (2):

The Muslim Brotherhood is an international Muslim Body which seeks to establish Allah's law in the land by establishing the spiritual goals of Islam and the true religion which are namely the following:

The need to inform the masses, Muslims and non-Muslims of Islamic teachings, explaining the signs in detail to those who understand the pure human nature upon which Allah has created man. Distinguish the universality of Islam, in addition to refuting fallacy.

Endeavor to purify the hearts and souls of men from evil and sin. Unify humankind into the fundamental principles of Islam and bringing closer the viewpoints of the Islamic sects. . .

Insist to liberate the Islamic Nation from the yoke of foreign rule, help safeguard the rights of Muslims everywhere and unite Muslims around the world.

The need to work on establishing the Islamic State, which seeks to effectively implement of the provisions of Islam and its teachings. (sic)

The sincere support for a global cooperation in accordance with the provisions of the Islamic Sharia, which would safeguard the personal rights, freedom of speech for active and constructive participation towards building a new basis of human civilization as is ensured by the overall teaching of Islam. (sic)

Article (3): The Muslim Brotherhood in achieving these objectives depends on the following means:

Make every effort for the establishment of educational, social, economic and scientific institutions and the establishment of mosques, schools, clinics, shelters, clubs as well as the formation of committees to regulate zakat affairs and alms. . .

As will be demonstrated in the coming pages, this is exactly what the Muslim Brotherhood has done in America. They have created thousands of organizations dedicated to achieving the MB's objectives.

The following statement of the By-Laws reveals the Brotherhood is not a non-violent political organization as some claim:

"The Islamic nation must be fully prepared to fight the tyrants and the enemies of Allah as a prelude to establishing the Islamic state."

This makes clear that when the time is right, the Muslim Brotherhood intends to use military force to overthrow our government.

This becomes important when we detail:

(1) the Special Section or military wing of the Brotherhood

(2) the use of their Islamic Centers as barracks

(3) the fact they have had jihadi training camps in America for at least 30 years.

The Muslim Brotherhood's official website is www.Ikhwanweb.com. In the spring of 2011, they took much of the historical information and their By-Laws off their site. Screen captures of the complete MB By-laws can now be found www.UnderstandingtheThreat.com.

KEY BOOKS AND DOCUMENTS:

Milestones, by Sayyid Qutb

Besides the founder of the Muslim Brotherhood, Hassan al Banna, the greatest ideologue for the Muslim Brotherhood was Sayyid Qutb. Qutb was an Egyptian who came to the U.S. in 1948 to study at the University of Colorado in Greeley.

Upon arriving back in Egypt in 1950, he wrote a series of articles in which he derided America's moral decay, and indicated the world is in need of Islamic revival. Soon thereafter, Qutb joined the Muslim Brotherhood Movement in Egypt.

In the 1950s, he was arrested along with many other Muslim Brothers in Egypt. While in jail, he wrote his seminal work, *Milestones*, which **operationalizes Islamic Law for the modern jihadi**, and is the centerpiece for jihadi organizations around the world.

In August 1966, Qutb was hanged by the Egyptian government for his association with and activities on behalf of the Brotherhood. He is a beloved martyr in the Muslim world today, and his complete writings can be found in nearly every Mosque bookstore and Islamic Center in the world.

Ayman al Zawahiri, the current leader of Al Qaeda, said of Qutb:

> "Sayyid Qutb's call for loyalty to Allah's oneness and to acknowledge Allah's sole authority and sovereignty was the spark that ignited the Islamic revolution against the enemies of Islam at home and abroad."

Qutb and *Milestones* are relevant and key to understanding the war in which we are engaged.

The 9/11 Commission Report recognized Qutb's importance:

> "In speeches and writings, the sightless [Abdel] Rahman, often called the "Blind Sheikh," preached the message of Sayyid Qutb's *Milestones*, characterizing the United States as the oppressor of Muslims worldwide and asserting that it was their religious duty to fight against God's enemies." (*9/11 Commission Report*, p72)

Qutb detailed the requirement in Islamic Law (Sharia) for all Muslims to adhere to Islamic Law. Qutb stated the world in general, and specifically the Islamic world, was in a state of "Jahiliyyah" or gross ignorance and unbelief, and the only way to get the Muslim world back to complete adherence to Islamic Law was through a series of "Milestones."

These "Milestones" would incrementally bring Muslims to the understanding of their requirement to wage jihad until the entire world is claimed for Islam. This is aligned with the Koranic concept of Abrogation or Progressive Revelation which is how Muhammad brought the first generation of Muslims to Islam – progressively in stages.

Three Koranic verses (2:106, 16:101, and 17:106) state the Koran was revealed in "stages." **Verses revealed chronologically were later abrogated/made null those which came before**. Therefore, verses such as "Let there be no compulsion in religion (2:256)" were abrogated by such verses as "Oh ye who believe, take not the Jews and the Christians as your friends and protectors, they are but friends and protectors to each other (5:51)" and "Fight and slay the unbeliever wherever you find them and lie and wait for them in every stratagem of war (9:5)."

Muhammad had approximately 23 years to bring the first generation of Muslims from Mecca (where all the revelations in the Koran are "peaceful") to Medina (where revelations progressively included defensive jihad, then offensive jihad for limited purposes, then offensive jihad as a permanent obligation upon all Muslims until the world is claimed for Islam.)

Because Qutb's *Milestones* follows Progressive Revelation it stands to reason that newly converted Muslims working with the Muslim Brotherhood will likely not know that jihad is "warfare" and is obligatory upon them. They will only be told this fact when the Muslim Brotherhood determines the individual is ready to go to the next Milestone.

This process of Progressive Revelation in *Milestones* is the **Radicalization Process** as seen by the U.S. law enforcement/intelligence/military communities.

Building Bridges? Qutb also wrote the following in *Milestones*:

> "The chasm between Islam and *Jahiliyyah* is great, and a bridge is not to be built across it so that the people on the two sides may mix with each other, but only so that the people of *Jahiliyyah* may come over to Islam."

This means that when an organization that is controlled by or allied with the Muslim Brotherhood in America works with your law enforcement, intelligence, or military organization, they do so only to subvert your mission.

Methodology of Dawah **by Shamim Siddiqi**

In 1989, the Brotherhood produced a key book entitled *Methodology of Dawah* by Shamim Siddiqi. The full title of this book as noted on the inside cover is *"Methodology of Dawah Ilallah in American Perspective"* (hereafter *Methodology*).

This book details how Muslim Brothers are to subvert American society with specific guidance and means to achieve their goals. "Dawah" is the requirement under Islamic Law for Muslims to "call" non-Muslims to Islam before waging jihad.

After 50 pages of the history of Islam, *Methodology*, like Qutb's *Milestones*, lays out in Chapter 4 a plan for the "Islamic Movement" in stages.

> "The stages of the Islamic Movement which was launched by the Prophet Muhammad (PBUH), and, as discussed in the previous Chapter, can be summarized as follows."

These six stages are then laid out:

1. Dawah

2. Organization or Jama'ah

3. Tarbiya (Training)

4. Peaceful Resistance

5. Migration – Hijrah

6. Final Stage (Armed Conflict)

Key Teachings Regarding Dawah:

> "This is the primary job...A comprehensive program will be presented, keeping in mind the prime objective to establish Allah's Deen in the society in which we are living."

Note: "Allah's Deen" is Islamic Law (Sharia).

Methodology emphasizes the importance of the "Final Stage:"

> "The Muslims of America have no option. They have to carry out the struggle in the way I have discussed in this book to the last breath of their lives until either the mission is accomplished or they pass on from this world as Mujahidin-fi-Sabil-Allah." (*Holy Warriors dying in the "Cause of Allah" or "Jihad"*).

It is important to note that Muslim Brotherhood organizations may advocate non-violence as a course of action today, but they will use

10

violence when they are ready and required to do so.

"It matters little for the Islamic Movement as to whether it takes one or many decades to make the ideology of Islam prevail over the mental horizon of the American people. The action must be taken now." (p. 68)

From Chapter 5, Survey of Present Dawah Activities in America:

"Dawah activities, at present, are being carried out by the Islamic Society of North America through I.T.C. (Islamic Teaching Center), the Muslim Community Center of Chicago, the Islamic Circle of North America, Nation of Islam, the Islamic Center of Washington and other organizations like these." (p. 73)

In detailing how "Afro-American people" are called to Islam and converted by the Da'ee (the one who calls the non-Muslim to Islam), Siddiqi states:

"Some rituals of religion and traditions of the Muslim Community are explained. A short account of the Prophet's life is presented, without the revolutionary aspect. When Islam is acceptable to the new entrants in this concocted or abbreviated form, the ceremony of Shahadah is performed with great reverence. A non-Muslim thus becomes a Muslim, obedient to Allah alone. **The revolutionary aspect of Islam is rarely brought before the new converts, as in most of the cases the Da'ee himself is not conversant with it.**" (p. 71, emphasis added)

Two key points are revealed here: (1) The Muslim Brotherhood Movement is a revolutionary movement; and (2) the Muslim Brotherhood lies to non-Muslims to get them to convert to Islam.

Finally, *Methodology* teaches that Da'ees are to deal with non-Muslims and call them to Islam using "pleasing words" and "in a pleasing and refined manner. Present the message in a respectable manner with dignity and patience." (.p 144) This teaches the Da'ees to speak softly and not become argumentative. This is an important lesson in helping determine when you have come across a MB trained Da'ee.

Toward a Worldwide Strategy for Islamic Policy

In November 2001, during a raid near Lugano, Switzerland at the residence of Youssef Nada, a senior Muslim Brother, a 14-page document dated 1982, entitled "*Toward a Worldwide Strategy for Islamic Policy*" was found. Now known as "The Project," the document details how the Muslim Brotherhood will subvert and take over Western nations, and bring

Muslim nations back to adherence to Islamic Law (Sharia). It should be noted that Youssef Nada was designated a terrorism financier by the U.S. Department of Treasury in 2001, as well as by the United Nations. Nada's business entities were also designated for funding terrorism. The document lists 12 "Points of Departure" detailing the Muslim Brotherhood's global strategy. They are quoted here:

Point of Departure 1: To know the terrain and adopt a scientific methodology for its planning and execution.

Point of Departure 2: To demonstrate proof of the serious nature of the work.

Point of Departure 3: To reconcile international engagement with flexibility at a local level.

Point of Departure 4: To reconcile political engagement and the necessity of avoiding isolation on one hand, with permanent education and institutional action on the other.

Point of Departure 5: To be used to establish an Islamic State; parallel, progressive efforts targeted at controlling the local centers of power through institutional action.

Point of Departure 6: To work with loyalty alongside Islamic groups and institutions in multiple areas to agree on common ground, in order to "cooperate on the points of agreement and set aside the points of disagreement".

Point of Departure 7: To accept the principle of temporary cooperation between Islamic movements and nationalist movements in the broad sphere and on common ground such as the struggle against colonialism, preaching and the Jewish state, without however having to form alliances. This will require, on the other hand, limited contacts between certain leaders, on a case by case basis, as long as these contacts do not violate the [shari'a] law. Nevertheless, one must not give them allegiance or take them into confidence, bearing in mind that the Islamic movement must be the origin of the initiatives and orientations taken.

Point of Departure 8: To master the art of the possible on a temporary basis without abusing the basic principles, bearing in mind that Allah's teachings always apply. One must order the suitable and forbid that which is not, always providing a documented opinion. But we should not look for confrontation with our adversaries, at the local or the global scale, which would be disproportionate and could lead to attacks against the dawa or its disciples.

Point of Departure 9: To construct a permanent force of the Islamic dawa and support movements engaged in jihad across the Muslim world, to varying degrees and insofar as possible.

Point of Departure 10: To use diverse and varied surveillance systems, in several places, to gather information and adopt a single effective warning system serving the worldwide Islamic movement. In fact, surveillance, policy decisions and effective communications complement each other.

Point of Departure 11: To adopt the Palestinian cause as part of a worldwide Islamic plan, with the policy plan and by means of jihad, since it acts as the keystone of the renaissance of the Arab world today.

Point of Departure 12: To know how to turn to self-criticism and permanent evaluation of worldwide Islamic policy and its objectives, of its content and its procedures, in order to improve it. This is a duty and a necessity according to the precepts of shari'a.

Like any good operational plan, this document includes three sections under each Point of Departure (PoD) – (a) Elements, (b) Procedures, and (c) Suggested Missions. The following are some key portions of some of the Points of Departure (PoD) and their significance to the strategy of the Islamic Movement and to us:

PoD 1, b-procedures: "Create observation centers in order to gather and store information for all useful purposes, if need be relying on modern technological methods."

On the ground, the Brotherhood establishes organizations for the purpose of intelligence collection and deception operations. For instance, search warrants have revealed lists of names of police officers and federal agents, vehicle descriptions and license plates of unmarked or covert vehicles, and other pertinent data inside the homes of jihadis/ Muslim Brotherhood operatives.

PoD 4, a-Elements: "To construct social, economic, scientific and health institutions and penetrate the domain of the social

13

services, in order to be in contact with the people and to serve them by means of Islamic institutions."

The Muslim Brotherhood Movement in the U.S. has established numerous social, scientific, and health institutions, including the Islamic Medical Association, the Association of Muslim Scientists and Engineers, the Association of Muslim Social Scientists, the Council on Islamic Education, and numerous other front groups designed to influence these professional communities and others as a part of the broader Islamic Movement.

> **PoD 5:** "To dedicate ourselves to the establishment of an Islamic state, in parallel with gradual efforts aimed at gaining control of local power centers through institutional action.
>
> a- Elements: To channel thought, education and action in order to establish an Islamic power [government] on the earth. To influence centers of power both local and worldwide to the service of Islam."

Everything the Muslim Brotherhood does, they do in pursuit of implementing Islamic Law and re-establishing the global Islamic State (Caliphate).

> **PoD 7:** "To accept the principle of temporary cooperation between Islamic movements and nationalist movements in the broad sphere and on common ground such as the struggle against colonialism, preaching and the Jewish state, without however having to form alliances."

On the international front, we see the Muslim Brotherhood in the form of Hamas working with Hizbollah (Shia) forces in combat in Iraq, as well as in policy and political subversion operations in Europe and the United States. The Muslim Brotherhood also works with Marxist/Communists groups in the U.S. in furtherance of anti-American causes (joint war protests etc.).

> **PoD 9:** "To construct a permanent force of the Islamic dawa and support movements engaged in jihad across the Muslim world, to varying degrees and insofar as possible."

The Islamic Society of North America is the Dawa entity for the Muslim Brotherhood in North America. They put out the "Call" to the non-Muslim world to invite them to Islam. This is a pre-requisite in Islamic Law to conducting jihad (warfare against non-Muslims).

The Hamas Covenant

The Islamic Resistance Movement, or Hamas, wrote and published its "Covenant" in 1988. Hamas was created out of the Palestinian Muslim Brotherhood. The MB is the parent organization of Hamas.

The heading over Article Two states: "The Islamic Resistance Movement's Relationship with the Moslem Brotherhood Group" and Article Two itself states, in part: "The Islamic Resistance Movement is one of the wings of the Moslem Brotherhood in Palestine. Moslem Brotherhood Movement is a universal organization which constitutes the largest Islamic movement in modern times."

KEY SUMMARY POINTS:

- All of the Muslim Brotherhood's published doctrine states the MB seeks to impose Shariah (Islamic Law) on the world through Jihad which it defines as "warfare against non-Muslims."

- The "Radicalization Process" as understood by U.S. law enforcement is actually a formal process of bringing Muslims from wherever they are to a place they will support and participate in jihad.

- The MB has detailed training programs they teach in U.S. Islamic Centers and other organizations they control.

- The MB is the parent organization of Hamas, a designated terrorist organization.

THE IMPLICATIONS OF THE HLF TRIAL

On Friday, August 20, 2004, a man and his family were driving across the Chesapeake Bay Bridge in Maryland. Baltimore County police officers observed the passenger filming the support structures of the bridge. When she saw the officers, she pulled the camera down. Believing this to be an investigative clue, the officers made a vehicle stop.

The driver was identified as Ismail Elbarasse, wanted on a Material Witness warrant in a Hamas case in Chicago, and linked to the leader of Hamas in the United States. He was taken into custody.

Subsequent to this, the FBI raided his home in Annandale, Virginia where they discovered the archives of the Muslim Brotherhood in North America. Many Muslim Brotherhood documents, financial records, photographs, videos, audio tapes, and a host of other items were discovered and seized.

Many of these documents were entered into evidence in the largest terrorism financing trial ever successfully prosecuted in U.S. history – The United States v The Holy Land Foundation for Relief and Development (hereafter "HLF").

At the time it was indicted by the federal government, HLF was the largest Islamic charity in the United States and sent more than $12 million overseas to fund Hamas. Hamas is designated as a Foreign Terrorist Organization (FTO) by the U.S. government.

In November 2008, in the Northern District of Texas (Dallas), HLF and its senior leadership were convicted of a total of 108 counts and sentenced to lengthy prison terms. The evidence presented and testimony given in this trial reveal several important points:

1. There is an "Islamic Movement" in the United States and it is led by the Muslim Brotherhood.

2. The Muslim Brotherhood is the parent organization of Hamas, designated a terrorist organization by the U.S. government.

3. The objective of the Muslim Brotherhood in America is to wage

"Civilization Jihad" to destroy America from within.

4. Many of the most prominent Islamic organizations in the U.S. were created by the Muslim Brotherhood and continue to serve their objectives.

5. The Islamic Society of North America, the largest MB organization in North America, is also a financial support entity for Hamas.

6. The North American Islamic Trust (NAIT), is the bank for the Muslim Brotherhood, and is also a financial support entity for Hamas.

7. As a result of a resolution issued by the International Muslim Brotherhood, the U.S. Muslim Brotherhood created a Palestine Committee/Section in the United States to raise money, conduct propaganda operations, and recruit men for Hamas. The U.S. MB originally created the Islamic Association for Palestine (IAP), the United Association for Studies and Research (UASR), and the Occupied Land Fund (OLF) which became the HLF, to be fronts for Hamas in America.

8. The Council on American Islamic Relations (CAIR), one of the most vocal opponents of all U.S. government counter-terrorism measures, purports to be a "civil rights" organization and was the fourth organization created by the U.S. Palestine Committee to be a front for Hamas in America.

We will now take a look at some of the key documents from the trial, decipher what they tell us about the Islamic Movement, and identify why this is important for law enforcement and intelligence professionals.

The World Underground Movement Plan

This is an undated document discovered by the FBI in the 2004 raid in Annandale, Virginia. It details a 5-Phase Plan for the Brotherhood to take over a country. It was discovered among the archives of the MB in America and is the "Concept of Operations" for their activities in the U.S. While this document was not entered as evidence in the HLF trial, it is important to start with it because it lays out the framework for the MB Movement here. Their actions taken here in the U.S. track with this phased plan. The following are direct quotes from this plan:

Phase One: Phase of discreet and secret establishment of elite leadership.

Phase Two: Phase of gradual appearance on the public scene... establishing a shadow government.

Phase Three: Escalation phase, prior to conflict and confrontation with the rulers.

Phase Four: Open public confrontation with the Government through exercising the political pressure approach...Training on the use of weapons domestically and overseas in anticipation of zero hour. It has noticeable activities in this regard.

Phase Five: Seizing power to establish their Islamic Nation.

In Phase Two, the Brotherhood plan states they have succeeded in subverting religious leadership, scholars, and gaining public sympathy for their Movement.

Additionally, they state they have a "Shadow Government" in place. The purpose of this Shadow Government is two-fold. Today, it is to influence decisions, policies, and the general direction of the government so it will be favorable towards their Movement.

It also acts as an intelligence gathering node until "Zero Hour." When "Zero Hour" comes and they attempt to overthrow the US government, the Shadow Government will be the leadership of the new Islamic Government.

Phase Four includes the admission by the Brotherhood that it conducts weapons training here in the United States "in anticipation of zero hour." As you will see in the next section, the MB has had jihad camps in the United States for over 30 years.

An Explanatory Memorandum: On the General Strategic Goal for the Group, 5/22/1991

This is the Muslim Brotherhood's strategic plan for North America. It was written by Mohammed Akram, who was the number two man in the Palestine Committee (Hamas) in the U.S. This document was approved by the governing bodies of the MB here – the Shura Council and the Organizational Conference. It was entered into evidence at the HLF trial (the largest Hamas trial ever successfully prosecuted in U.S. history), and was stipulated to by the defense counsel.

On the first substantive page of the Explanatory Memorandum in section "One," the Brotherhood lays out the foundation upon which it was written. It makes clear: (1) this document was approved by the governing bodies of the MB in North America; (2) the MB seeks to present Islam as an

18

alternative civilization to ours; (3) they intend to establish an Islamic State here; (4) "Settlement" is a process they are using to fulfill their objectives here; and (5) the Islamic Circle of North America is an integral part of this Movement.

The Process of Settlement

When the Muslim Brotherhood came to America, they came with a process of how to achieve their stated goals of establishing an Islamic State (Caliphate) under which Islamic Law (Sharia) would be the law of the land. According to this strategic document, the "Process of Settlement" is a "Civilization Jihadist Process" and a responsibility. This process is meant to transform a society, American society, from what it is now to an Islamic Society.

> **Four: The Process of Settlement:**
>
> In order for Islam and its Movement to become "a part of the homeland" in which it lives, "stable" in its land, "rooted" in the spirits and minds of its people, "enabled" in the lives of its society and has firmly-established "organizations" on which the Islamic structure is built and with which the testimony of civilization is achieved, the Movement must plan and struggle to obtain "the keys" and the tools of this process in carry out this grand mission as a "Civilization Jihadist" responsibility which lies on the shoulders of Muslims and - on top of them - the Muslim Brotherhood in this country.
> -*Copied portion of "An Explanatory Memorandum"*

The MB Mission in America

In the excerpt below from An Explanatory Memorandum, we see that the Muslim Brotherhood states their mission is to wage "Civilization Jihad" to destroy us by both our own and Muslim hands. These are their words.

> **4- Understanding the role of the Muslim Brother in North America:** The process of settlement is a "Civilization-Jihadist Process" with all the word means.
>
> *The Ikhwan must understand that their work in America is a kind of grand Jihad in eliminating and destroying the Western civilization from within and "sabotaging" its miserable house by their hands and the hands of the believers so that it is eliminated and Allah's religion is made victorious over all other religions.*

Without this level of understanding, we are not up to this

challenge and have not prepared ourselves for Jihad yet. **It is a Muslim's destiny to perform Jihad and work wherever he is and wherever he lands until the final hour comes, and there is no escape from that destiny** except for those who chose to slack. But, would the slackers and the Mujahedeen be equal. -*Copied portion of "An Explanatory Memorandum," emphasis added*

The Process of Settlement, as previously stated, is Civilization Jihad by OUR hands. They seek to get our leadership – political, religions, media, university/college presidents and boards, and law enforcement / intelligence / military professionals to do their bidding for them.

How this works:

Remember, we are dealing with a counterintelligence and espionage issue more than we are a counterterrorism" issue.

When the Muslim Brotherhood approaches a pastor/priest/rabbi, General, Assistant Director of DHS or FBI, State Legislator, Member of Congress, police chief, member of the media, or a university president, they do so wearing suits, with a pleasant demeanor, and generally offer something to the ones they are approaching.

Some of the Muslim Brothers are trained intelligence officers from other countries, and they seek to convince U.S. leaders to use them as the "go to" guys for all questions about Islam and counterterrorism strategies. This approach is working well for them.

Over time, these U.S. leaders begin making decisions, creating policy, drafting training programs, and recruiting new employees as a result of the advice and counsel he/she is getting from their Muslim Brotherhood advisor/friend. The evidence indicates that when this happens, the training, policies, and decision-making all favors the Muslim Brotherhood. It also numbs organizations to the danger the MB poses, puts forward an understanding of Islamic Law that has no basis in fact, and seeks to dampen all law enforcement responses to real threats.

The Islamic Centers

When the Muslim Brotherhood arrived in the United States in the 1950s, they originally settled in Illinois, Indiana, and Michigan. This explains why Chicago is the hub for Hamas in America, why Plainfield, Indiana is the home of the Islamic Society of North America, and why Detroit and Dearborn, Michigan are centers of significant Muslim Brotherhood and jihadi activity.

When the MB "settled" they did so in small groups of men who, over time, patiently grew their circle of influence, built infrastructure and organizations, and conducted Dawah – the "Call" to Islam.

Initially, the Muslim Students Association (MSA) was a significant gathering point for the Brotherhood work because many of the original Muslim Brothers were of the age of university students. The MSAs are still points of recruitment and work for the MB today. Remember, the MSA was the first national Islamic organization in America – and it was created by the Muslim Brotherhood. As these concentric circles of influence grew, so did the Muslim Brotherhood's areas of control and power. They continued to recruit, raise money, and influence the key leaders in the society (religious, media, political, education).

The central point around which the Process of Settlement is driven is the Islamic Center. The Brotherhood builds Islamic Centers across America to be the "axis" of their Movement and to "supply (their) battalions." These Centers are not simply places of worship. On the contrary their own documents say it is a place for all activity surrounding the MB's mission here and the place from which they will launch their military assault at "Zero Hour."

The Brotherhood specifically states:

> "Meaning that the 'center's' role should be the same as the 'mosque's' role in the time of Allah's prophet...when he marched to 'settle' the Dawa in its first generation in Madina." (sic)

Mohammed used the mosque in Medina as a place to gather the community, store food/water, house/train jihadis, teach about Islam, store weapons and ammunition, plan and strategize military campaigns, launch attacks, and pray. The Muslim Brotherhood says their Islamic Centers in North America are used for the same purpose. In other words, the Muslim Brotherhood Islamic Centers serve as the military outposts for the violent jihad in North America. **Today there are over 2,100 Islamic Centers in America - in all 50 states.**

> 17- Understanding the role and the nature of work of "The Islamic Center" in every city with what achieves the goal of the process of settlement: The center we seek is the one which constitutes the "axis" of our Movement, the "perimeter" of the circle of our work, our "balance center", the "base" for our rise and our "Dar al-Arqam" to educate us, prepare us and supply our battalions in addition to being the "niche" of our prayers.

21

This is in order for the Islamic center to turn- in action not in words- into a seed "for a small Islamic society" which is a reflection and a mirror to our central organizations. The center ought to turn into a "beehive" which produces sweet honey. Thus, the Islamic center would turn into a place for study, family, battalion, course, seminar, visit, sport, school, social club, women gathering, kindergarten for male and female youngsters, the office of the domestic political resolution, and the center for distributing our newspapers, magazines, books and our audio and visual tapes.

In brief we say: we would like for the Islamic center to become "The House of Dawa" and "the general center" in deeds first before name. As much as we own and direct these centers at the continent level, we can say we are marching successfully towards the settlement of Dawa in this country.

Meaning that the "center's" role should be the same as the "mosque's" role during the time of Allah's prophet, Allah's prayers and peace be upon him, when he marched to "settle" the Dawa in its first generation in Madina from the mosque. he drew the Islamic life and provided to the world the most magnificent and fabulous civilization humanity knew.

This mandates that, eventually, the region, the branch and the Usra turn into "operations rooms" for planning, direction, monitoring and leadership for the Islamic center in order to be a role model to be followed.

-*Copied portion of "An Explanatory Memorandum"*

Sunni & Shia Islamic Centers

Relatively little research and investigation is required to determine that a large number of the Sunni Islamic Centers in America are directly affiliated with the Islamic Society of North America (ISNA) and/or the North American Islamic Trust (NAIT), thus providing more evidence they are controlled by the Muslim Brotherhood and hostile to the community in which they are located. The Shia Islamic Centers should be investigated for ties to the Iranian government via front organizations such as the Alavi Foundation, raided by Federal Agents in 2011. Shia Centers with these ties are also hostile to your community.

The Organizations

The last page of the MB strategic document ("An Explanatory Memorandum") is a list of organizations working in the Muslim Brotherhood's Islamic Movement here in North America, and therefore, are all hostile to the United States.

It should be noted that this document is over 20 years old, yet some of the organizations listed are still the most prominent Islamic organizations in existence today.

They include:

- Muslim Students Association (MSA)
- Islamic Society of North America (ISNA)
- North American Islamic Trust (NAIT) which is the "bank" for the Muslim Brotherhood in America
- Fiqh Council of North America (FCNA), formerly the ISNA Fiqh Committee, acting as the Majlis al Shura for the Brotherhood in North America
- Islamic Circle of North America (ICNA)
- Islamic Association of Palestine (IAP) whose leaders now run the Council on American Islamic Relations (CAIR)
- International Institute for Islamic Thought (IIIT)
- and others.

See the document on the next page

From a copied portion of "An *Explanatory Memorandum*":

"A list of our organizations and the organizations of our friends [Imagine if they all march according to one plan!!!]"

1-ISNA	= ISLAMIC SOCIETY OF NORTH AMERICA
2-MSA	= MUSLIM STUDENTS' ASSOCIATION
3-MCA	= THE MUSLIM COMMUNITIES ASSOCIATION
4-AMSS	= THE ASSOCIATION Of MUSLIM SOCIAL SCIENTISTS
5-AMSE	= THE ASSOCIATION Of MUSLIM SCIENTISTS AND ENGINEERS
6-IMA	= ISLAMIC MEDICAL ASSOCIATION
7-ITC	= ISLAMIC TEACHING CENTER
8-NAIT	= NORTH AMERICAN ISLAMIC TRUST
9-FID	= FOUNDATION FOR INTERNATIONAL DEVELOP-MENT
10-IHC	= ISLAMIC HOUSING COOPERATIVE
11-ICD	= ISLAMIC CENTERS DIVISION
12-ATP	= AMERICAN TRUST PUBLICATIONS
13-AVC	= AUDIO-VISUAL CENTER
14-IBS	= ISLAMIC BOOK SERVICE
15-MBA	= MUSLIM BUSINESSMEN ASSOCIATION
16-MYNA	= MUSLIM YOUTH OF NORTH AMERICA
17-IFC	= ISNA FIQH COMMITTEE
18-IPAC	= ISNA POLITICAL AWARENESS COMMITTEE
19-IED	= ISLAMIC EDUCATION DEPARTMENT
20-MAYA	= MUSLIM ARAB YOUTH ASSOCIATION
21-MISG	= MALASIAN [sic] ISLAMIC STUDY GROUP
22-IAP	= ISLAMIC ASSOCIATION FOR PALESTINE
23-UASR	= UNITED ASSOCIATION FOR STUDIES AND RE-SEARCH
24-OLF	= OCCUPIED LAND FUND
25-MIA	= MERCY INTERNATIONAL ASSOCIATION
26-ISNA	= ISLAMIC CIRCLE OF NORTH AMERICA
27-BMI	= BAITUL MAL INC
28-IIIT	= INTERNATIONAL INSTITUTE FOR ISLAMIC THOUGHT
29-IIC	= ISLAMIC INFORMATION CENTER

Investigative Example

National media covered a story about a mosque being built in Murfreesboro, Tennessee. Here is a screen capture of the mosque's website.

Dr. Ossama Mohamed Bahloul, a graduate of Al-Azhar University in Cairo, Egypt, where he received a Bachelor of Arts in Islamic Studies (Usool el Din) ranking top 4 in a class of 200. He is certified in authentic recitation of the Quran "Hafs an 'Asim" method by his honor Sheikh Mahmoud Attiah Zayed.

He completed his (MS) with high honors in which his thesis was the establishment of a Da'awah curriculum aimed at secularists, atheists, Christians, Jews, and Muslims, and completed his PhD in Comparative Religious Studies in which his thesis is the Critique of Christian issues within Will Durant's "The Story of Civilization" and achieved the honor of excellence with the request for the publishing of his thesis.

He has been the Imam of the Islamic Society of Southern Texas in Corpus Christi, Texas, as well as a visiting Imam for the Islamic Center of Irving in Irving, Texas and the Islamic Center of Darmishtat in Frankfurt, Germany. Dr. Ossama has conducted Islam 101 presentations on college campuses and churches. He has been an organizer of town hall meetings, open houses, and community breakfasts with civic and religious leaders.

This is not just a "Mosque" – it is an Islamic Center. The website identifies the Imam of the Islamic Center of Murfreesboro as Dr. Ossam Mohamed Bahloul. In reading Dr. Ossama Bahloul's bio, we discover he has been the leader of Muslim Brotherhood front organizations around the world, including the Islamic Society of Southern Texas; the Islamic Center of Irving (Texas); and the Islamic Center of Darmishtat in Frankfurt, Germany.

What is most unusual is that Dr. Bahloul is a graduate of Al-Azhar University in Cairo, Egypt where he ranked 4th out of 200 other Islamic Legal Scholars. Al-Azhar University is the most prominent school of Islamic Jurisprudence in the world, and it is the oldest. It is the gold standard for Islamic Legal Doctrine in the Muslim world. [Reminder: These are LEGAL SCHOLARS not pastors, priests, or rabbis].

25

A logical investigative question must follow the discovery of this information: if Dr. Bahloul has demonstrated himself to be one of the top Islamic Legal Scholars of Islamic Law (Sharia) from the top University in the world for Islamic Jurisprudence, why was he not sent to Egypt, Jordan, Turkey, or the UAE? Why was he not sent to London, Spain, or France?

No, he was sent to Murfreesboro, Tennessee. There is a reason for this. The Muslim Brotherhood is not prone to random decision-making. As a law enforcement officer, investigator or intelligence analyst, this specific information reveals the MB is targeting Tennessee with senior scholars and leaders. The question to be asked is "WHY?"

Other Key MB Organizations

Muslim American Society (MAS)

The three founding directors of MAS were three of the most senior Muslim Brothers in the U.S. at the time. Ahmad Elkadi was the General Guide (Leader) of the Muslim Brotherhood in America from the mid-1980s to the mid-1990s. Jamal Badawi is a prominent Muslim Brother serving in senior positions with MB groups, an unindicted co-conspirator in the HLF trial, and is specifically named in the MB's strategic document.

Omar Soubani was on the Board of Directors for the MB in North America (see Elbarasse Address book, later in this Section). Additionally, senior MAS official Shaker Elsayed stated that "Ikhwan members founded MAS," (Chicago Tribune, 9/19/2004) and federal prosecutors stated that "MAS was founded as the overt arm of the Muslim Brotherhood in America (US v Sabri Benkahla)."

Muslim Public Affairs Council (MPAC)

The Muslim Public Affairs Council was formed out of the Islamic Center of Southern California, a Muslim Brotherhood front organization, and was created with the help of Maher Hathout, a protégé of MB founder Hassan al Banna. It serves as a significant Muslim Brotherhood public relations front, and has a strong presence in Hollywood and within government entities. MPAC authored *"Building Bridges to Strengthen America: Forging an Effective Counterterrorism Enterprise between Muslim Americans and Law Enforcement"* which is being used by law enforcement and homeland security agencies in the U.S. today as a guide for working with the Muslim community.

Implementation Manual (1991-1992)

This MB document was discovered during the 2004 FBI raid in Annadale, VA and implements their strategy (An Explanatory Memorandum). This lists the goals and assigns tasks to ensure that the Strategy is achieved in the US.

Department/ Committee	Goals to be accomplished through the years (1991-1992)
0 – Executive Office	1 – Developing the Group Center to include a general and organization offices and a secretariat. 2 – Identifying the problems facing the Group and working on resolving them. 3 – Strengthening and building relations with those working in the arena. 4 – Realization of and improvement on the idea of the Islamic conference. 5 – Arriving at a specific definition of the relationship with ICNA. 6 – Developing (3) Islamic Centers and supporting them to become fronts for Brotherhood work. 7 – Announcing field leadership for the Group in the (3) coming years.
1 – Education	8 – Concentrating on the practical side of Education. 9 – Education through dealing and associating. 10 – Caring for the spiritual side of education. 11 – Moving the educational work to public work circle. 12 – Offering educational care for the English speakers and the sisters.
2 – Organizations	13 – Elevating the faith and intellectual levels of the Ikhwan. 14 – Paying attention to public work and recruitment. 15 – Raising the administrative capacity of the Department and Regional secretariat. 16 – Putting new standards for commitment in place.
3 – The Sisters	17 – Elevating the level of expertise in the administrative and educational Department for the sisters. 18 – Developing women leadership at the public and private levels. 19 – Elevating the level of performance and awareness among the Masul's for the Regions and Usra organizations. 20 – Elevating the sisters' belief, intellectual and activity levels. 21 – Caring for the wives of the Ikhwan and raising the level of recruitment. 22 – Paying attention to public work and to communities. 23 – Developing the work of the female youth and children.

4 – The Youth	41 – Advancing the quality and usefulness of the activities performed by the organizations and guiding them. 42 – Elevating the levels of coordination among the organizations and systems of the Group and utilizing them. 43 – Elevating the levels of coordination among organizations and organizing the distribution of roles. 44 – Accomplishing administrative stability and embodying the organizational work in the organization. 45 – Accomplishing financial self sufficiency for these organizations. 46 – Developing work and increasing its efficiency in the Arab Islamic community sectors.
5 – The Political	28 – Awareness and education. 29 – Preparing the statements and offering suggestions with political positions. 30 – Offering a study about options of Islamic political work in the American arena. 31 – Starting the work on forming a general Islamic opinion about the worries of the Muslim community here.
6 – Local Work	32 – Restoring the existence of the Group in ISNA. 33 – Developing ISNA. 34 – Establishing field leadership for ISNA. 35 – Developing school projects in the communities. 36 – Intra community work. 37 – Conducting future, strategic studies. 38 – Supporting individual initiatives and projects. 39 – Developing the work with ICNA and similar Islamic organizations. 40 – Finding new financial sources for public work.
7 – Youth Organizations	41 – Advancing the quality and usefulness of the activities performed by the organizations and guiding them. 42 – Elevating the levels of coordination among the organizations and systems of the Group and utilizing them. 43 – Elevating the levels of coordination among organizations and organizing the distribution of roles. 44 – Accomplishing administrative stability and embodying the organizational work in the organization. 45 – Accomplishing financial self sufficiency for these organizations. 46 – Developing work and increasing its efficiency in the Arab Islamic community sectors.
8 – Financial	47 – Continuing financial gain and controlling expenditures. 48 – Developing the Group's financial resources. 49 – Developing the work of the Department.
9 – Social	50 – Continuing financial support. 51 – Accomplishing administrative stability. 52 – Continuing the publishing of the social bulletin.
10 – Matrimonial	53 – Providing necessary information. 54 – Simplifying the marriage process and solving its related problem.

11 – The Dawa	55 – Establishing a registered, official umbrella for the work of the Dawa Committee 56 – Delivering the message of Islam to non-Muslims 57 – Contacting Islamic Centers to present them the services of the Dawa Committee. 58 – Providing Dawa bulletins to the Islamic Centers. 59 – Assisting the Islamic Centers in spreading the Dawa.
12 – South America	60 – Completing the special studies related to Muslim demographics, especially the observant among them. 61 – Determining the organizational level. 62 – Strengthening the ties and supporting the activities specific to the regular brothers. 63 – Multiplying the number of Ikhwans in Brazil. 64 – Creating strong relationships with the committed Groups in the area.
13 – Security	65 – Developing the prepared rules and referring them to the Office for approval and implementation. 66 – Publishing a security bulleting for the Group. 67 – Preparing a study about the effect of the Gulf War on the Group and suggesting solutions. 68 – Developing the security aspect of a limited number of the leading brothers.
14 – The Palestine Committee	69 – Improving and accomplishing financial, administrative and job stability of the organizations. 70 – Reaching an investment ceiling of (500) thousand dollars. 71 – Reaching a donations ceiling of (1.5) million dollars. 72 – Preparing and training (20) Ikhwans for working in the American arena upon their return. 73 – Highlighting (10) brothers to become political and media symbols in the American arena. 75 – Establishing (3) branch offices for the Association (IAP). 76 – Facilitating the establishment of a political office, women organization, youth organization and a medical union
15 – The Center and Secretariat	77 – Reaching a general secretariat devoted to the Group. 78 – Attaining a secretarial that is devoted to the Group. 79 – Rearranging the center to incorporate the organizational division. 80 – Arranging the work of the center from the legal and security aspects.
16 – Foreign Affairs	81 – Establishing a relations network with those working for Islam. 82 – Exchanging expertise and visits with Europe. 83 – Finding formats for collaboration with the existing Islamic organizations.
17 – Mercy Foundation	84 – Continuing advertising and calling for fund collection (Zakat and sacrifices) and its distribution. 85 – Contributing to supporting the afflicted in the Gulf. 86 – Preparing for the final calculations for the past fiscal year. 87 – Preparing a vision for projects of continuous nature.

Board of Directors, U.S. Muslim Brotherhood

Source: Elbarasse Phonebook – Evidence at US v HLF trial, Dallas, 2008

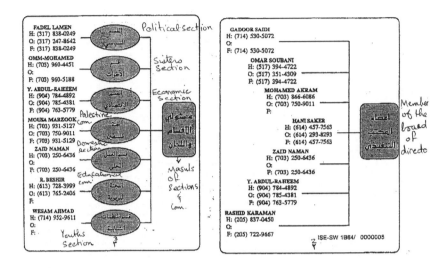

Key MB Leaders

Source: MB's "Preliminary Vision for Future Leadership" – 1988
"Apparatuses" is the Section, and Columns 1-3 List
Muslim Brothers Leading that Section+

The Apparatuses	1	2	3
The Shura	Al-Qadi	Al-Jabri	Subani
The office	Al-Qadi	Mousa	Subani
Gaf Dha Ta	Gaddour	Akram	Nasr
Institutions	Subani	Bassam	Tariq
Financial	Nazim	Al-Haydar	Salah
Political			
The sisters	Abd-al-Mannan	1	2
The planning	Akram	Tariq	Subani
Legal	Walid	Mousa	
(10)The Court	Hanooti	Elmezain	Adam
(11)Special Committee	Jamal	Bassam	Mousa
(12)Social	Elmezain	Sadoun	Hamid
(13)Curricula	Tariq	Akram	Subani
(14)Security	Izzat	Khalil	M. Salah
(15)Capabilities	Wisam	Walid	Safwat
(16)Palestine C.	Mousa	Subani	Akram
(17)D. Regions	Hani	Nasr	Safwan
(18)ISNA	Zaki	Dawud	Imtiyaz
(19)MAYA	Hattab	Shukri	Husayn
(20)MSA	Ghulam	Riyad	Sati
(21)MISG	Husni	Adrus	Abd-al-Latif
(22)NAIT	Bassam	Jamal	Zaki
(23)MYNA	Badiyya	Abu Karam	Nidal
(24)AMSS	Abu Solayman		
(25)AMSE	Bartuma		
(26)IMA	Wahhaj Ahmad		
Schools and Education			
Communities and Centers			
Youth			
Economic C.			

CAIR is Hamas

"I am in support of the Hamas Movement more than the PLO."
CAIR Founder Nihad Awad – Barry University, March 1994

"Islam isn't in America to be equal to any other faith, but to become dominant...The Koran, the Muslim book of scripture, should be the highest authority in America, and Islam the only accepted religion on Earth."
-CAIR Founder Omar Ahmad, Argus Newspaper,
Fremont, CA, July 4th, 1998

The Council on American Islamic Relations (CAIR) was created in 1994 by the Palestine Committee in the United States (Hamas) to be the "Political" arm of Hamas here in America. As was previously mentioned, Hamas (The Islamic Resistance Movement) is the Muslim Brotherhood in Palestine, and is a designated Foreign Terrorist Organization by the United States government.

Evidence seized during the 2004 FBI raid in Annandale, VA where the MB archives were discovered detail that in 1992 the International Muslim Brotherhood created Palestine Committees in every nation where the MB had a presence at the time "to make the Palestinian cause victorious and to support it with what it needs of media, money, men and all of that."

The U.S. Palestine Committee initially created three organizations to be Hamas nodes in America: The United Association for Studies and Research (UASR), the Islamic Association of Palestine (IAP), and the Occupied Land Fund (OLF) which became the Holy Land Foundation for Relief and Development (HLFRD or simply HLF). As previously noted, HLF was convicted in 2008 for sending over $12 million overseas to Hamas, a US designated terrorist organization.

In this section, facts and evidence will be laid out to demonstrate that CAIR was the fourth organization created by the U.S. Palestine Committee (Hamas) to recruit jihadis, raise money, and gain media favor for Hamas in America. The Leaders of CAIR, Nihad Awad and Omar Ahmad, were in leadership positions in the IAP prior to the creation of CAIR. The Chairman overseeing HLF, UASR, and the IAP, was Musa Abu Marzook, the number three man for Hamas in the world at the time and the leader of the Palestine Committee in the U.S. Marzook was designated a terrorist by the U.S. government in 1995.

1993 Philadelphia Meeting of the U.S. Palestine Committee

The following from the Government's Trial Brief in US v HLF is important because the MB/Hamas methodology revealed that its operations overseas are nearly identical here in the U.S:

> "In October 1993, less than one month after the public signing of the Oslo Accords, approximately 20 members of the Palestinian Committee gathered together in Philadelphia, Pennsylvania to discuss how best to proceed in light of the Olso Accord...

> The FBI obtained a warrant from the Foreign Intelligence Surveillance Court to monitor the meeting, which lasted approximately three days. During the meeting, the participants openly discussed the problems that the Oslo Accords posed for achieving their objectives. **The United States was fertile ground for fundraising and propaganda, offering the essential Constitutional protections which afforded the freedom to operate** (emphasis added).

> Since the United States had publicly positioned itself behind the peace process, the attendees were concerned that disclosure of their true purpose would threaten their established infrastructure by aligning them with what they knew was a terrorist organization.

> Attendees were admonished not to mention "Hamas," but rather to refer to it as "Samah," which is Hamas spelled backwards. Attendees questioned how they could continue their quest to defeat the peace process without being viewed as "terrorists."

> They discussed their concern that the peace process would attract Palestinian support and further complicate their ultimate goal of creating an Islamic state throughout Israel. They agreed that they must operate under an ostensible banner of apolitical humanitarian exercise in order to continue supporting Hamas' vital social recruitment effort.

> In order to facilitate their continued support of Hamas, the attendees discussed the method by which they could provide financial support without an overt alignment with Hamas. That method involved supporting institutions, organizations and programs in the West Bank and Gaza aligned with the Hamas movement. Attendees identified several organizations and zakat committees as 'ours.'"

In official documents, the FBI stated the Philadelphia meeting was "a meeting...among senior leaders of Hamas, the HLFRD, and the IAP" (FBI Action Memo from Counterterrorism Assistant Director Dale Watson) and "all attendees of this meeting are Hamas members." (FBI analysis of the Philadelphia conference entered into evidence at HLF trial)

Present at this meeting of Hamas leaders: Nihad Awad and Omar Ahmad, Founders of CAIR

Internal Muslim Brotherhood documents entered into evidence at the HLF trial reveal Omar Ahmad is on the Executive Committee of the Palestine Committee in the U.S. (ie Hamas).

A document entitled "Important phone and fax numbers (Palestine Section/America)" was discovered in the 2004 FBI raid in Annandale, VA. In this one page document were the names of Palestine Committee Members (Hamas) in the U.S. The names of "Nihad Awad" and "Omar Yehya" aka Omar Ahmad (Founders/Leaders of CAIR) were on this list.

Because of evidence and testimony at the HLF trial in Dallas, CAIR was named as one of the unindicted co-conspirators in this case (ie there is enough evidence to indict CAIR but the government chose not to do so at this time).

Reminder: HLF is the largest terrorism financing and Hamas trial ever successfully prosecuted in U.S. history. Specifically, CAIR was identified as a member of the Palestine Committee in the United States, meaning they are part of the MB's Hamas network in America.

CAIR, along with ISNA and NAIT, filed memorandums with the Federal Court in Dallas seeking to have their names removed from the unindicted co-conspirator list in the HLF case. The prosecution filed a memorandum stating:

> "Shortly after Hamas was founded in 1987, as an outgrowth of the Muslim Brotherhood, *Govt. Exhibit 21-61*, the International Muslim Brotherhood ordered the Muslim Brotherhood chapters throughout the world to create Palestine Committees, whose job it was to support Hamas with "media, money, and men." *Govt. Exhibit 3-15*. The U.S. Muslim Brotherhood created the U.S. Palestine Committee, which documents reflect was initially comprised of three organizations: the OLF (HLF), the IAP, and the UASR. **CAIR was later added to these organizations.**" (emphasis added)

In his ruling, Federal Judge Jorge Solis stated: **"The Government has produced ample evidence to establish the associations of CAIR, ISNA and NAIT with HLF, the Islamic Association for Palestine (IAP), and with Hamas."**

The judge ordered CAIR, ISNA, and NAIT to remain on the unindicted co-conspirator list. A three-judge Federal Appellate panel unanimously upheld this decision.

In the fall of 2008, the FBI cut off all ties with CAIR because of their ties to Hamas.

In a letter from Assistant Attorney General Ronald Weich to U.S. Congresswoman Sue Myrick (NC) dated 2/10/2010 in response to a question by the Congresswoman asking the Department of Justice to brief all Members of Congress on the implications of the HLF trial, AAG Weich stated:

"Enclosed are four copies of the trial transcripts on CD-ROM that contain testimony and other evidence that was introduced in that trial which demonstrated a relationship between CAIR, individual CAIR founders, and the Palestine Committee. Evidence was also introduced that demonstrated a relationship between the Palestine Committee and Hamas, which was designated as a terrorist organization in 1995."

KEY SUMMARY POINTS

- At the time it was indicted, the Holy Land Foundation for Relief and Development (HLF) was the largest Islamic charity in America.

- US v HLF was the largest Hamas and terrorism financing case ever successfully prosecuted in U.S. history.

- HLF and its leaders were convicted and given lengthy prison sentences.

- Evidence entered at the HLF trial revealed there is an "Islamic Movement" in the United States led by the Muslim Brotherhood with the objective of waging "Civilization Jihad" to overthrow our government and replace it with an Islamic government.

- The Muslim Students Association (MSA) was the first national

Islamic organization in America and was founded by the Muslim Brotherhood in 1962. Today there are over 600 MSA chapters at colleges and universities across the U.S.

- A majority of Islamic organization in America, and the most prominent ones, were created by the U.S. Muslim Brotherhood.

- The Islamic Society of North America (ISNA) and the North American Islamic Trust (NAIT) are financial support entities for Hamas.

- The Council on American Islamic Relations (CAIR) was created by the U.S. Muslim Brotherhood to be a Hamas entity here.

- The MB's "Islamic Centers" are the "axis" of their Movement here in North America from which they launch jihad.

MB IS A JIHADI ORGANIZATION – VIOLENCE IS A TOOL

As its own doctrine clearly indicates, the Muslim Brotherhood is a Revolutionary organization, and the Islamic Movement led by the Muslim Brotherhood is a Revolutionary movement which seeks to destroy all non-Islamic governments and institute a global Islamic state (Caliphate) under which Islamic Law (Sharia) is the law of the land. The means for doing this is "Jihad" which the Muslim Brotherhood only defines as "warfare."

> **MB By-Laws:** *"The Islamic nation must be fully prepared to fight the tyrants and the enemies of Allah as a prelude to establishing the Islamic State."*

> **Underground Movement Plan:** *"Training on the use of weapons domestically and overseas in anticipation of 'Zero Hour.' It has noticeable activities in this regard." (from Phase IV)*

> **MB Creed:** *"...Jihad is our way and martyrdom is our highest aspiration."*

> **An Explanatory Memorandum:** *"The center we seek is the one which constitutes the 'axis' of our movement, the 'perimeter' of our circle of work...to prepare us, educate us, and to supply our battalions..."*

> **The previous "Supreme Guide" or Leader of the International Muslim Brotherhood (Mohammed Akef) was interviewed on May 22, 2008 in the Arabic media about his thoughts on Osama bin Laden and responded:** *"Most certainly he is a Mujahid. I do not doubt his sincerity in resisting occupation for the sake of Allah Almighty."* (NOTE: A "Mujahid" is a holy warrior. The leader of the International Muslim Brotherhood praised the leader of Al Qaeda.)

> **Hamas Covenant:** *"The Islamic Resistance Movement is one of the wings of the Muslim Brotherhood in Palestine."* (NOTE: Hamas is a designated Foreign Terrorist Organization by the US)

As was previously detailed, the Muslim Brotherhood was violent in Egypt from the very beginning of its founding. The founder of the MB, Hassan al Banna, was targeted by Egyptian Security Services because of the bombings, assassinations and other violent operations perpetrated by the Muslim Brotherhood in Egypt.

As the Brotherhood's Doctrine makes clear, violence is an inherent part of who they are. It is a tool to achieve their objectives when it suits them.

As is factually detailed below, the MB has jihadi networks and training camps in America, and has an Internal Security Apparatus to protect itself against law enforcement and intelligence agencies here as well.

During the 2004 FBI raid in Annandale which uncovered the MB archives in North America, a recording was discovered of a senior Muslim Brother speaking to a group of Muslim Brothers in 1981 in Missouri.

Zeid al Noman, the leader (Masul) of the MB's Executive Office, spoke to fellow Muslim Brothers and detailed how the MB came to America, how it set up and utilized the Muslim Students Association (MSA), and how the MB grew over the first two decades here in America. He laid out the MB's objectives, the road forward, and then answered questions.

In the below transcript "Ze" is Zeid Noman and "UM" are Muslim Brothers asking questions. From this exchange, three key points are revealed:

1. The Muslim Brotherhood has its "Special Section" (Military Wing) in America

2. The Muslim Brotherhood has an internal security apparatus here in the U.S.

3. The Muslim Brotherhood has had jihadi training camps in America since 1981

From the transcript:

> Um: **By "Securing the Group", do you mean military security?** And, if it is that, would you explain to us a little bit the means to achieve it.
>
> Ze: **No, Military work is listed under "Special work". "Special work" means military work.** Securing the Group" is the Groups' security, the Groups' security against outside dangers. For instance, to monitor the suspicious movements on the…, which exist on the American front such as Zionism, Masonry…etc. Monitoring the suspicious movements or the sides, the government bodies such as the CIA, FBI…etc, so that we find out if they are monitoring us, are we not being monitored, how we can get rid

of them. That's what is meant by "Securing the Group".

[Later in the Q & A]

Um: You mentioned that **there is a weapons training at the Ikhwans' camps** but I did not see that at all in the mid-southern region camps. So, would you explain to us the reasons.

Ze: By Allah, the first thing is that you thank Allah and praise him because you found a camp to meet in. You know that, for instance, Oklahoma has become a blocked area for you. You cannot meet in it in the first place, right? Then, the nature…What? [Unintelligible talk from the audience] Yes, I'm sorry. I thought…, OK. My brothers, according to what we learned…, to what I learned, in Oklahoma they started to be strict about letting Muslims use the camps. They would ask them, for instance, to submit their name and they would ask you to bring an ID or something to prove your name. I learned that they were going on a picnic recently, a trip, and the police came asking each person to give…, to present a…er, to show his ID or even his visa. These harassments exist then in the state of Oklahoma, for instance. And these are among the reasons which made our brothers . . . have their camps here in Missouri. Right, my brother? Then, the circumstances which a region goes through are the ones which determine. In some of the regions when they go to a camp, they take two things, **they would request a camp which has a range, a shooting range and one which has a range to shoot, one which has a range which they use for shooting.** You would find that in some of the camps. They would get an advance permit for that. I mean, I don't know the possibility of having these camps here and also whether the pressure which exists in Oklahoma, and whether they will **have a weapons training in the other regions**…, these harassments might continue, I mean, become contagious to the other regions.

A reminder to the reader: the Muslim Brotherhood's 5-Phase plan for overthrowing America, the *"World Underground Movement Plan,"* states in Phase IV:

"Training on the use of weapons domestically and overseas in anticipation of zero hour. It has noticeable activities in this regard."

While this is not the totality of all the doctrine and statements of the MB and its leadership, it is clear the MB is hostile to the United States and plans to use violence when it suits their objectives.

KEY SUMMARY POINTS

- The Muslim Brotherhood's published doctrine states they will wage jihad to achieve their objectives.

- The Muslim Brotherhood's Special Section – military wing – is here in the United States.

- The MB has an internal security apparatus to protect its interests against U.S. law enforcement and intelligence gathering.

- The MB has dozens of jihadi training camps in the U.S. and has had them here since at least 1981.

SECTION 6:

ISLAMIC LAW

The Enemy's Stated Threat Doctrine

The overwhelming majority of individuals with whom the United States military is engaged and nearly every Muslim arrested for an act or planned act of "terrorism" state they are fighting "Jihad" in the "Cause of Allah" in order to establish an Islamic State (Caliphate) under Islamic Law - known as Sharia.

In order to accurately understand what this means, the professional duty of those with national security responsibilities is to know how jihad is understood by the enemy when mapped against "Jihad" as defined in Islamic Law, and to understand what Islamic Law is and its role in Islam. Without this knowledge, the enemy cannot be accurately identified, targeted and defeated.

Framework for Sharia (Islamic Law)

Islam defines itself as a complete way of life – social, cultural, religious, military, and political - governed by Islamic Law (Sharia). Islamic Law is real law which governs all affairs of Muslims. The Sharia, as it is called, is primarily derived from the Koran and the Sunnah (the collection of the Hadith and the Sira).

For Muslims, the Koran is considered the "uncreated word of Allah." This means Muslims believe everything in the Koran was directly revealed to the Prophet Muhammad by Allah (the god in Islam) and, therefore, cannot be changed.

The 114 Suras (Chapters) in the Koran are arranged by size from largest to smallest (not chronologically), with the exception of the first Sura which is introductory. Sura 2 is the largest and Sura 114 is the smallest. **This is critical to understanding the Koran because peaceful verses revealed to Muhammad in Mecca were abrogated (overruled) by the verses commanding warfare which came chronologically later in Medina** (see section on "Abrogation").

In Islam, the Prophet Muhammad is the most perfect example of a human being. All that he did and said is to be modeled by Muslims. The Hadith is the collection of all of the practices, sayings, and traditions of the Prophet Muhammad.

The Sira are the authorized sacred biographies of Muhammad.

Hadith: There are hundreds of thousands of Hadith, which have been evaluated by Islamic Legal Scholars (Jurists) as to their validity based on their chain of transmission from the Prophet to the reporting author. The Hadith are categorized as mawdu (false), munkar (ignored), da'if (weak), hasan (good), sahih (sound), and mutawatir (strongest, most rigorously authenticated).

There are six sacred Hadith scholars and they are, in rank order, Bukhari, Muslim, Abu Dawud, al-Sugra, Tirmidhi, and Ibn Majah. Bukhari and Muslim are considered the most reliable. In Islamic Law, Mutawatir Hadith from Bukhari rises to the level of being second only to the Koran.

Dar al Harb / Dar al Islam

In Islam, the entire world is divided into the Dar al Harb, "the house or abode of war," and the Dar al Islam, "the house or abode of peace." All lands which are not under Muslim control and ruled by Sharia, are considered Dar al Harb – enemy lands. "Harbi" means enemy personnel, or inhabitants of the Dar al Harb. Therefore, under Islamic Law, all persons not in Islamic Lands ruled by Sharia are enemy persons. All lands occupied by Muslim forces at any time in history are considered "Muslim Lands" for all time.

Ijma (Scholarly Consensus)

Ijma is one of two critical legal concepts in Islamic Law, especially Sunni Islamic law. Ijma, or "scholarly consensus" means that when the Mujtahids (senior Islamic Legal Jurists) of a particular time period gather together, rule on points of Islamic Law, and unanimously agree on these points of law, the ruling becomes a permanent part of Islamic Law for all time and can never be changed. The core issues within Islam have been ruled upon by scholarly consensus in Islamic Law – specifically the issues of Jihad, relations between Muslims and non-Muslims, and the requirement for the establishment of the Caliphate.

> "When the four necessary integrals of consensus exist, the ruling agreed upon is an authoritative part of Sacred Law that is obligatory to obey and not lawful to disobey." [*Umdat al Salik, The Classic Manual of Islamic Sacred Law*, al-Misri, b7.2]

A way to recognize when this "absolute" standard is being applied is when writings state "this is a matter over which all the scholars agree," "there is no disagreement among the scholars," or similar language.

Abrogation

Abrogation is a second legal concept in Islamic Law critical to understanding the underpinnings of the threat doctrine. Simply put, abrogation means that anything revealed to Muhammad chronologically later in the Koran abrogates or overrules anything which came earlier.

Abrogation is a Koranic concept which comes from three verses in the Koran (2:106, 16:101, 17:106) meaning, from the perspective of Islam, it came from god and, therefore, can never be amended or nullified. Chronologically, the last Sura in the Koran to discuss relations with non-Muslims is Sura 5, and the last Sura to discuss Jihad is Sura 9.

Relations with non-Muslims [From Sura 5: Final word on this issue in the Koran]

It is a permanent command in Islam for Muslims to hate and despise Jews and Christians and not take them as friends. This comes from both the Koran as well as from the sacred hadith scholars Bukhari and Muslim.

> "Oh ye who believe! Take not the Jews and the Christians for your friends and protectors; they are but friends and protectors to each other. And he amongst you that turns to them for friendship is of them. Verily Allah guideth not the unjust." [*Koran 5:51*]

> The Prophet said, "The hour [of judgment] will not come until the Muslims fight the Jews and kill them. It will not come until the Jew hides behind rocks and trees. It will not come until the rocks or the trees say, 'O Muslim! O servant of God! There is a Jew behind me. Come and kill him. Except for the gharqad, which is a tree of the Jews.'" [*Sacred Hadith, Bukhari, 103/6, number 2926*]

> Allah's Apostle said, "By Him in Whose Hands my soul is, surely (Jesus,) the son of Mary will soon descend amongst you and will judge mankind justly (as a Just Ruler); he will break the Cross and kill the pigs and there will be no Jizya (i.e. taxation taken from non Muslims)." [*Sacred Hadith, Bukhari, vol 4, book 55, number 657*]

Note: this last Hadith states that the Muslim prophet Jesus will return to earth with Muhammad and will cast all Christians to hell and kill all Jews in order that Muslims may go to 'Paradise.'

43

Jihad [From Sura 9: Final word on this issue in the Koran]

Jihad is a permanent obligation on the Muslim community until the entire world is made the Dar al Islam.

Jihad is the sixth Right of Pure Worship between god and man – the first five being the "pillars" of Islam.

The Koranic Basis for Jihad

Islamic Law provides three options for 'People of the Book' (those who had a holy book prior to Muhammad): (1) They may convert to Islam; (2) they may be killed; or (3) they may pay the jizya (non-Muslim tax) and be subjugated to Islamic Law having little rights as non-Muslims under the law. Pagans and others who had no holy book prior to Muhammad must either convert to Islam or be killed.

> "Fight and slay the unbelievers wherever ye find them, and lie in wait for them in every strategem of war. But if they repent, and establish regular prayers and practice regular charity, then open the way for them; for Allah is Oft-forgiving, Most Merciful." [*Koran 9:5, the Sura of the Sword*]

> "Fight those who believe not in Allah nor the Last Day, nor hold that forbidden which hath been forbidden by Allah and His Apostle, nor acknowledge the religion of truth, even if they are of the people of the Book, until they pay the jizya with willing submission, and feel themselves subdued." [*Koran 9:29*]

Jihad has only ever been defined in Islamic Law as 'warfare against non-Muslims':

> "Jihad means to war against non-Muslims...signifying warfare to establish Islam" and is "obligatory for every Muslim" [*Umdat al Salik, Classic Manual of Islamic Law (Shafi), Ahmad ibn Naqib al-Misri, d. 1368.*]

> "War...is obligatory on men who are free, have attained puberty, who find the means for going to war, are of sound health, and are neither ill nor suffer from a chronic disease...the jurists agreed, with respect to the people who are to be fought, that they are all of the polytheists, because of the words of the Exalted, 'And fight them until persecution is no more, and religion is all for Allah." [*The Distinguished Jurist's Primer (Maliki), Ibn Rushd, d. 1198*]

> "'Fight the unbeliever wherever you find them and lie and wait for them in every strategem of war...' 'I have been commended to

fight the people until they testify that there is no deity worthy of worship except Allah and that Muhammad is the Messenger of Allah...' This honorable Ayah (verse) 9:5 (Koran) was called the Ayah of the Sword, about which Ad-Kahhak bin Muzahim said, "It abrogated every agreement of peace between the Prophet and any idolator, every treaty, and every term.' " [*Tafsir of ibn Kathir, d. 1373*]

"Jihad is a communal obligation...Jihad is determined till the Day of Judgment...'Then shall ye fight, or they shall submit (Koran 48:16)' When the Muslims commence battle, and they have surrounded a city or a fort, they are to invite the inhabitants to accept Islam...If they respond positively, they are to refrain from fighting them, due to the attainment of the purpose. If they refuse, they are to invite them to the payment of jizyah, and this is what the Prophet ordered the commanders of the armies to do for it is one of the consequences upon the conclusion of battle...if they reject the invitation, they are to seek the help of Allah and engage them in combat." [*Al-Hidayah, A Classic Manual of Hanafi Law, Primary Hanafi Text since 767 AD*]

"Fight in the name of God and in the 'path of God.' Combat only those who disbelieve in God...Whenever you meet your polytheist enemies, invite them to adopt Islam. If they do so, accept it and let them alone...if they refuse then call upon them to pay the jizya. If they do, accept it and leave them alone..." [*The Islamic Law of Nations, Shaybani's Siyar*]

"The jurists have distinguished four different ways in which the believer may fulfill his jihad obligation: by his heart; his tongue; his hands; and by the sword...the believers are under the obligation of sacrificing their 'wealth and lives' in the prosecution of war." [*War and Peace in the Law of Islam, Majid Khadduri, 1955*]

"The word jihad is most often associated with the act of physically confronting evil and wrong-doing...if anyone dies in a Jihad they automatically go to Paradise. A Shaheed or Martyr, is described this way by Allah, 'Don't think that those who were killed in Allah's Cause are dead. No they are alive, finding their bounty in the presence of their Lord...the Law of the Land is the Sharia of Allah...the duty of the Muslim citizen is to be loyal to the Islamic State.'" [*"What Islam is All About" (most popular Islamic junior high school text in the U.S. - printed in English), 1997*]

"The Holy Koran spelt out the object of the divine war against Paganism soon after it commanded the Muslims to take recourse to fighting. 'And fight them on until there is no more tumult or oppression...'The Holy Koran wishes to see the Muslim armies always in an uppermost, dominating and commanding position over those of their adversaries....Terror struck into the hearts of the enemies is not only a means, it is the end in itself. Once a condition of terror into the opponent's heart is obtained, hardly anything is left to be achieved. It is the point where the means and the end meet and merge...Psychological dislocation is temporary; spiritual dislocation is permanent...To instill terror into the hearts of the enemy, it is essential, in the ultimate analysis, to dislocate his Faith. An invincible Faith is immune to terror...This rule is fully applicable to nuclear as well as conventional wars." [*The Quranic Concept of War by Brigadier General SK Malik, Pakistani Army; Forward by Chief of Staff Pakistani Army Zia ul Haq (who became President of Pakistan), and Preface by Advocate General of Pakistan Brohy who calls this a "Restatement" of the Islamic Law of War. This was written in English in 1979 and is DOCTRINE in Pakistan*]

"Jihad as warfare must be fought when the Muslim community has the ability to do so. Even when this is not possible, a standing requirement exists to wage jihad via the pen or with words. At a minimum, however, all Muslims are under permanent obligation to hate and despise the non-Muslim rule." [*Jihad of the Heart*].

Truces

In Islamic Law, Muslim fighting forces may only call for a truce when they are in a position of weakness and **require time to resupply and rebuild forces.** It is a grave concern because it entails nonperformance of jihad.

"Truces are permissible, not obligatory. The only one who may effect a truce is the Muslim ruler of a region (or his representative)...There must be some interest served in making a truce other than mere preservation of the status quo. Allah Most High says, 'So do not be fainthearted and call for peace, when it is you who are the uppermost.' [*Koran 47:35*]

"Interests that justify making a truce are such things as Muslim weakness because of lack of numbers or materiel, or hope of an enemy becoming Muslim." [*Umdat al Salik, Book O: Jihad, o9.16*]

46

Lying

Islamic Law specifically allows, and in some cases obliges, Muslims to lie to non-Muslims if doing so furthers the cause of Islam.

> "The Prophet said, 'He who settles disagreements between people to bring about good or says something commendable is not a liar.'" [*Sacred Hadith, Bukhari & Muslim*]

> "I did not hear him (the Prophet Muhammad) permit untruth in anything people say except for three things: war, settling disagreements, and a man talking with his wife or she with him." [*Sacred Hadith, Muslim*]

> "Speaking is a means to achieve objectives...**it is permissible to lie if attaining the goal is permissible...and obligatory to lie if the goal is obligatory.**" [*Imam Abu Hamid Ghazali, Renowned Islamic Jurist, quoted in Umdat al Salik, Sacred Islamic Law, Book R: Holding One's Tongue, r8.2*]

Slander

In Islamic Law, anyone who says anything about Muslims, Islam, or the Prophet, that Muslims dislike is guilty of "Slander." The punishment for slander in Islamic Law is death. This applies to oral and written statements, and even drawings.

> Slander in Islamic Law means "to mention anything concerning a person that he would dislike." [*Umdat al Salik, r2.2*]

> "As for talebearing, it consists of quoting someone's words to another in a way that worsens relations between them." [*Umdat al Salik, r2.3*]

> "The above define slander and talebearing. As for the ruling on them, it is that they are unlawful, by the **consensus of Muslims.**" [*Umdat al Salik, r2.4*]

Talebearing

> "Talebearing is unlawful...Talebearing is a term that is usually applied only to someone who conveys to a person what another has said about him." [*Umdat al Salik, Book R: Holding One's Tongue, r3.0*]

Informing on Another Muslim / Spying

Under Islamic Law, it is a crime for Muslims to inform or spy on another Muslim.

"The Prophet said, 'Let none of my Companions inform me of anything another of them has said...'" [*Umdat al Salik, r5.1*]

"Anyone approached with a story, who is told, "So-and-so says such and such about you,' must...not let what has been said prompt him to spy or investigate whether it is true, for Allah Most High says, 'Do not spy' [Koran 49:12]; and not to do himself what he has forbidden the talebearer to do, by relating it to others." [*Umdat al Salik, r3.1(5-6)*].

Do Not Assist Police

"It is not permissible to give directions and the like to someone intending to perpetrate a sin...Giving directions to wrongdoers includes: (1) Showing the way to policemen and tyrants..." [*Umdat al Salik, r7.1*]

Apostasy

Apostasy is when a Muslim leaves Islam. This is a capital crime and is punishable by death. There is a requirement for the Muslim to be advised of his error before he is killed.

"Leaving Islam is the ugliest form of unbelief and the worst." [*Umdat al Salik, o8.0*]

"When a person who has reached puberty and is sane voluntarily apostatizes from Islam, he deserves to be killed. In such a case, it is obligatory for the caliph (or his representative) to ask him to repent and return to Islam. If he does, it is accepted from him, but if he refuses, he is immediately killed...There is no indemnity for killing an apostate since it is killing someone who deserves to die." [*Umdat al Salik, o8.1-o8.4*]

Zakat (mandatory financial payments required of all Muslims)

"It is obligatory to distribute one's zakat among eight categories of recipients (meaning that zakat goes to none besides them), one-eighth of the zakat to each category." [*h8.7, ZAKAT, Umdat al Salik*]

"The 8 categories listed in the aforementioned book of Islamic Law are: (1) The Poor; (2) Those Short of Money; (3) Zakat

Workers; (4) Those Whose Hearts are to be Reconciled; (5) Those Purchasing Their Freedom; (6) Those in Debt; (7) Those Fighting for Allah; and (8) Travellers Needing Money.

Under category (7) Those Fighting for Allah, Islamic Law specifically states: "Those Fighting for Allah. H8.17. The seventh category is those fighting for Allah, meaning people engaged in Islamic military operations for whom no salary has been allotted in the army roster (but who are volunteers for jihad without renumeration). They are given enough to suffice them for the operation, even if affluent; of weapons, mounts, clothing, and expenses (for the duration of the journey, round trip, and the time they spend there, even if prolonged)."

It should be noted that the *Umdat al Salik* or *"Reliance of the Traveller"* is published in Beltsville, Maryland in English and can be found in many Islamic Centers/Mosque bookstores across America and on popular book sales websites.

A number of certifications are listed in the front of *"Reliance"* testifying to its authoritative nature in Islamic law. Specifically, a letter signed by the President of the International Institute for Islamic Thought (IIIT) and the President of the Fiqh Council of North America, both known Muslim Brotherhood entities and authorities for Islamic law in North America, states:

> "There is no doubt that this translation is a valuable and important work, whether as a text book for teaching Islamic jurisprudence to English-speakers, or as a legal reference for use byscholars, educated laymen, and students in this language...the translation presents the legal questions in a faithful and precise idiom that clearly delivers the complete meaning in a sound English style."

For investigators and intelligence analysts: the Islamic Law contained within *Reliance of the Traveller* has been approved by the Muslim Brotherhood as doctrine. Therefore, when the MB uses words like "Jihad" or "Truce" those words only mean what Islamic Law would have them mean.

Regarding Zakat, this also means that when Muslim Brotherhood entities collect Zakat, they have formally declared that at least 1/8 of all money they raise goes to support JIHAD – what we call TERRORISM. That is an articulable fact which goes towards Probable Cause.

KEY SUMMARY POINTS

- All Islamic doctrine defines Islam as a "complete way of life" – social, cultural, political, military, and religious – all governed by Shariah (Islamic Law).

- 100% of authoritative published Islamic Law obliges the Islamic community to wage Jihad until the entire world is subordinated to Islamic Law.

- 100% of authoritative Islamic Law only defines Jihad as "warfare against non-Muslims."

- 100% of authoritative Islamic Law obliges Muslims to lie to non-Muslims when the objective is obligatory. Jihad is obligatory.

- Zakat is obligatory giving by Muslims. Islamic law mandates that 1/8 of all Zakat goes to Jihad.

- Authorities in Islam are legal scholars, jurists, and judges.

UNDERSTANDING THE LANGUAGE OF THE JIHADI

As was mentioned in the previous section, Islamic Law is the enemy threat doctrine and it is what the enemy seeks to impose on the world. Members of the Law Enforcement, Military, and Intelligence Communities must remember to use Islamic Law as the "filter" by which they can understand what the enemy means when he speaks, writes, or acts. The table below is a list of common words adherents to Islamic Law use:

WORD USED	THE WORD'S MEANING IN ISLAMIC LAW
Justice	The Justice provided to people living under Islamic Law
Freedom	Freedom from man-made or secular laws
Terrorism	Killing a Muslim Without Right. Under Islamic Law there are specific reasons for a Muslim to be killed (e.g. Apostasy). Under Islamic Law, if a Muslim is killed for a reason not specified under the law, the person who killed the Muslim must also be killed. This applies to US forces in Afghanistan, Iraq, and elsewhere.
Innocents	Only Muslims are innocent under Sharia
Jihad	Warfare against non-Muslims
Suicide	Killing oneself. Unlawful under Sharia.
Martyrdom	Dying in jihad. The only way under Sharia a Muslim is guaranteed entry into Paradise. Muslims who blow themselves up while killing non-Muslims in jihad are Martyrs, not "suicide bombers."

Peace	When the entire world is subordinated to Islamic Law and living under the global Islamic State (Caliphate) with an Islamic Ruler (Caliph), the entire world will be under the "Dar al Islam" or the house of Islam and Peace, and there will be Peace on earth.
Human Rights	The "rights" afforded to people living under Islamic Law. In an official document (Cairo Declaration) served to the United Nations in 1993 by the Organization of the Islamic Conference (OIC) – the largest international body second only to the UN – the heads of state and kings of every Muslim nation on earth (57 states including Palestine) agreed the entire Muslim world understands the term "human rights" only as Islamic Law understand it, and no other source of law can define "human rights" outside of Islamic Law (Sharia). This means when someone who is adherent to Sharia (e.g. a Muslim Brother) uses the phrase "human rights," he only means the imposition of Islamic Law.

Example

After the arrest of a member of the Muslim community in the U.S., the Imam of a local MB-controlled Islamic Center speaks to the media. The Imam says, "We are dismayed by the arrest of this young man. We categorically condemn terrorism, we call for the protection of all innocent people, and we want to see human rights spread throughout all of America so we can live in peace."

Translated using Islamic Law as the filter, this actually means: "We are upset this man was arrested by infidel forces. We condemn the killing of Muslims without right, we call for your government to protect all Muslims, and we want to see the world subordinated to Islamic Sharia so we can live in peace under the global Islamic State in the Dar al Islam."

SECTION 8:

MB INFRASTRUCTURE
IN AMERICA

*"We are in a country which understands no language other than
the language of the organizations, and one which does not respect
or give weight to any group without effective, functional, and strong
organizations."*

From the Muslim Brotherhood's Strategic Memorandum

It is noteworthy to recall that the **first** national Islamic organization
created in the United States – the Muslim Students Association (MSA) –
was created by the Muslim Brotherhood. From that time in 1962, nearly
all of the prominent Islamic organizations in America were formed out of
the MSA, and many admit to this on their websites.

At the time it was indicted, the Holy Land Foundation (HLF) was the
largest Islamic charity in the United States, and it was convicted in U.S.
Federal Court of being a Hamas entity which funneled over $12 million
to Hamas, a designated terrorist organization. These are two important
data points to remember going forward. The Brotherhood's Movement in
America is significant and deeply rooted.

The graph on the next page reveals the number of Islamic charities in the
United States and the years in which they were created. This data comes
from Internal Revenue Service Forms (990) which record data from non-
profits in America. The graph reveals there is a direct relationship between
Muslim Brotherhood doctrine and the creation of Muslim Brotherhood
organizations.

Specifically in the graph, it can be seen that after the Islamic Society of
North America (ISNA) was created and formed in the early 1980s, a large
number of Islamic non-profits were created – many of these are local
subsidiaries of ISNA called "The Islamic Society of (locale)."

In 1991, an upturn in the number of Islamic charities created begins and
never diminishes. 1991 is the year the Muslim Brotherhood published
their strategic document, *An Explanatory Memorandum*, followed by the

American Islamic Organizations
Historical Rate of Foundation/Year

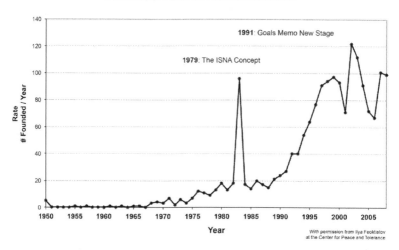

With permission from Ilya Feoktistov
at the Center for Peace and Tolerance

MB's Implementation Manual (dated 1991/1992), which lists the types of organizations needed to further the MB's Movement here in America. A large number of non-profits were then created, and continue to be created, which fit the mold of the MB's needs detailed in their strategic documents.

In fact, between 60 and 120 Islamic non-profits are created each year in the United States, and today there are over 2,000 non-profit Islamic organizations in America registered with the IRS.*

Not all of these organizations are a part of the Brotherhood's Movement in the U.S., but a large number are and can be tracked to known MB front groups. This number does not include for-profit Islamic organizations controlled by the Muslim Brotherhood, MB lobbying organizations, nor covert MB organizations.

Large numbers of prominent Muslim Brotherhood organizations are not included in this list as well. As of the date of the printing of this Handbook:

- Only 70 of the MSA's 600 plus chapters in the United States are registered with the IRS as non-profit organizations.* The MSA's website lists 206 chapters in the U.S. but a review of University and College websites reveal that nearly every major university and college in America has an MSA on or near campus.

- Only 470 "Islamic Centers" / "Mosques" / "Masjids" out of 2,106 (as of April 2012) are registered with the IRS as non-profit organizations.* Investigation and testimony before the

54

U.S. Congress demonstrates that as much as 80% of the Islamic Centers in America are controlled by the Muslim Brotherhood. A conservative estimate for our purposes is 50% which gives us 1,053 Islamic Centers controlled by the MB in the U.S. today.

- The subsidiaries of the Islamic Society of North America across the country (e.g., "Islamic Society of Greater Houston" etc) number approximately 230.

- The Muslim American Society (MAS) and Hamas (DBA CAIR) do not have all their Chapters listed with the IRS as non-profit organizations*. Between these two organizations, there are approximately 75 offices around the nation.

- Many MB organizations do not have words in their names obviously identifying them as Islamic organizations (e.g. Holy Dove Foundation) and so the results of searches of IRS 990 forms will not reveal them unless it is known to the researcher.

Using conservative estimates, and just using a handful of known Muslim Brotherhood entities, we see the MB has over 2,000 organizations working each day across America serving its ultimate objective of overthrowing the government of the United States. This reflects a massive infrastructure for this hostile movement, which exists in neighborhoods across America.

*Source: www.Guidestar.com using key search words identifying the organizations as Islamic

PENETRATION OF
THE U.S. SYSTEM

IN THEIR OWN WORDS
Muslim Brotherhood Leaders on the MB Mission in America:

"If only Muslims were clever politically, **they could take over the United States and replace its constitutional government with a caliphate**. If we were united and strong, we would elect our own emir and give allegiance to him. Take my word if eight million Muslims unite in America, the country will come to us." - - *Imam Siraj Wahhaj, first Muslim Imam to offer prayers at U.S. House of Representatives*

"We have a chance, in America to be the moral leadership of America...It will happen, it will happen praise [Allah] the Exalted. I have no doubt in my mind. It depends on me and you, either we do it now or we do it after a hundred years, **but this country will become a Muslim country**." - *Abdurahman Alamoudi, Islamic Advisor to President Clinton, created Muslim Chaplain Program for Department of Defense,*

Evidence reveals the Muslim Brotherhood has been successful in penetrating the U.S. security apparatus at all levels, and placed Muslim Brothers at key positions inside the government.

By gaining positions inside U.S. law enforcement and intelligence organizations, the Muslim Brotherhood is able to insert false and confusing information into our analytical and decision-making process (Denial and Deception) while gathering intelligence at all levels.

The following are a few of the hundreds of examples of significant penetrations by the Muslim Brotherhood/Al Qaeda inside the U.S. system.

These men are all Muslim Brothers living and operating in the United States.

Abdurahman Alamoudi

- Islamic Advisor to President Clinton
- "Goodwill Ambassador" for U.S. State Department
- Founded/Led nearly two dozen of the largest Islamic organizations in North America, including DOD Muslim Chaplain Program
- Arrested in 2003 in London (UK) with $340,000 cash received from Libya for global Jihad
- Involved in plot with 2 UK-based AQ operatives to kill Saudi Crown Prince (who became King) Abdullah
- Al Qaeda Financier. Hamas/MB operative
- Pled guilty in Eastern District of VA in 2004 - serving lengthy sentence in federal prison

Siraj Wahhaj

- First Imam to offer prayers in the U.S. House of Representatives
- Prominent Islamic scholar and lecturer
- Imam of the Al Taqwa mosque in Brooklyn, NY
- Executive Director, Muslim Alliance in North America (MANA)
- National Board Member of Hamas (CAIR)
- Board of Advisors, American Muslim Council (AMC)
- Unindicted co-conspirator, 1993 World Trade Center Bombing
- Character witness for Abdel Rahman ("Blind Sheikh") at WTC bombing trial in 1990s
- Vice President of ISNA

Imam Anwar al-Awlaki

- Imam of the Dar al Hijrah Islamic Center in Falls Church, VA
- Trained Muslim Chaplains for the U.S.
- Lectured at the U.S. Capitol in 2002 on the life of the prophet Mohammed and Islam – filmed for a PBS documentary
- Spoke at a Pentagon event in February 2002 to senior officials
- Hailed by U.S. media as "new generation of Muslim leader" (NY Times) who can "build bridges between Islam and the West" (NPR)
- Senior Al Qaeda recruiter and leader of AQ in Yemen
- Gave Islamic legal advice and authorization for Jihad to US Army Major Nidal Malik Hasan (Ft. Hood shooter), Umar Farouk Abdulmutallab ("underwear bomber") and others
- Targeted and Killed in September 2011 by US Government

Muzammil Siddiqi

- Director of the Islamic Society of Orange County (CA)
- Founding Member, Council of Mosques (US & CANADA)
- Invited by President Bush to read a prayer at the 9/11 Memorial Service at the National Cathedral in 2001
- Hosts Law Enforcement (LAPD & LA Sheriff), U.S. Attorney, Members of Congress and others (2012)
- Former President and Board Member, ISNA
- Chairman, Fiqh Council of North America
- Chairman, North American Islamic Trust (NAIT)

Imam Mohamed Magid

- Executive Director, All Dulles Area Muslim Society (ADAMS) Center, Sterling, VA
- President, Islamic Society of North America (ISNA)
- Islamic Advisor to U.S. State Department
- On the DHS Homeland Security Advisory Group
- Works with the National Security Council
- Teaches DHS, FBI, and CIA on building trust in the community between law enforcement and Muslims.

Salam al Marayati

- Founder & Executive Director, Muslim Public Affairs Council (MPAC)
- 1999 – Marayati's nomination to National Commission on Terrorism withdrawn once it was revealed he supports acts of terrorism
- Al Marayati described Hizbollah attacks as "legitimate resistance"
- MPAC hosts terrorists as speakers at their conferences from Al Qaeda and Hamas (eg Alamoudi, Sami al Arian)
- MPAC condemns the FBI arrests of terrorists in America as potential civil rights issues against Muslims
- MPAC's Hollywood bureau works to ensure Muslims are not portrayed in a derogatory manner in American films

Parvez Ahmed

- Currently serves as the Human Rights Commissioner for Jacksonville, Florida
- Professor, University of North Florida
- Presented the Civil Liberties Award by the ACLU in 2002
- Former Chairman of the Board, Hamas in the US (CAIR)
- Speaks at conferences of Muslim Brotherhood front groups in the United States

Sheikh Muhammad al Hanooti

- Renowned Islamic Scholar
- Council Member, Fiqh Council of North America
- Imam of the Dar al Hijrah Islamic Center in Falls Church, VA, 1995-1999
- FBI Report: "Al Hanooti collected over $6 million for support of Hamas"
- Unindicted Co-Conspirator in largest terrorism financing and Hamas trial in U.S. history (US v HLFRD)
- Unindicted Co-Conspirator in 1993 World Trade Center Bombing
- Trustee and Former Director, Islamic Association of Palestine (IAP), a Hamas front organization.

Suhail Khan

- Served in the White House until 9/11/01
- Former Assistant to U.S. Transportation Secretary Mary Peters for Policy matters
- Received the Department of Transportation's Gold Medal for his superb service (2007)
- Former Policy Director for U.S. Representative Tom Campbell (1999)
- Washington Lobbyist for Microsoft
- Board of Directors, American Conservative Union
- Former Member of the Board, Islamic Free Market Institute
- Senior Fellow, Institute for Global Engagement
- Son of Mahboob Khan, one of the original Muslim Brotherhood leaders in the United States and founder of the Muslim Students Association, ISNA, and the Muslim Communities. Note: ISNA has an annual award called the "Mahboob Khan Award."
- After his death in 2001, the official English language website for the International Muslim Brotherhood (ikhwanweb.com) posted a tribute to Mahboob Khan
- Malika Khan, Suhail's mother, is on the Executive Committee for the San Francisco Bay Area chapter for Hamas (CAIR)
- Suhail openly praises the work of his father and mother's efforts on behalf of the Muslim ummah in America
- Al Qaeda financier Abdurahman Alamoudi presented Suhail Khan with an award in 2001 and praised him for following in his father's footsteps
- Suhail is the Chairman of Muflehun, serving with Mohamed Magid, the President of ISNA
- In a 1999 speech at the national ISNA conference, Suhail Khan stated, "Islamophobia" should be resisted with "all the determination, all the resources, all the unyielding vigilance of the believing mujahid (holy warrior)."
- Publicly stated there is no Muslim Brotherhood movement in the United States

Nihad Awad

- One of the leading voices and recognizable figures in America for "Islamic issues"
- Served on Vice President Al Gore's Civil Rights Advisory Panel
- Works with and briefs numerous law enforcement agencies and Congress and their staffs
- Has appeared on numerous television and radio outlets
- Executive Director, Hamas in the US (Council on American-Islamic Relations, CAIR)
- Former Director at the Islamic Association for Palestine (IAP) a now-defunct Hamas entity in the U.S.

Sheikh Kifah Mustapha

- Imam of the Mosque Foundation in Bridgeview, IL The Mosque Foundation supported Global Relief Foundation, the Holy Land Foundation, and the Benevolent Foundation (all three are Al Qaeda or Hamas support entities).
- Chairman of the Board, The Koran Institute MAS, Chicago
- Named by the U.S. government as a member of the Muslim Brotherhood's "Palestine Committee" meaning he is a member of Hamas
- Member of the Arab American Religious Council of Greater Chicago
- Registered agent for the Holy Land Foundation (Hamas) in Illinois: 1990s to 2001

Sayeed Sayyid

- Internationally recognized Islamic scholar and speaker on interfaith dialogue
- Advisor to Members of Congress, U.S. Department of State, several U.S. agencies, and others
- Addressed the First International Conference of Imams and Rabbis in Brussels in 2005
- Received Lifetime Achievement Award from the Catholic Heritage Foundation
- Member of Board of Trustees, Council for a Parliament of the World's Religions
- National Director, ISNA
- Former President, Muslim Students Association
- Former General Secretary AMSS

KEY SUMMARY POINTS

- Key Islamic advisors to the U.S. government are easily identified as members of the Muslim Brotherhood's Movement.
- The primary purpose of having these jihadis in these roles is to insert false information into our decision-making process, gather intelligence on our activities, and minimize our preparation and response to real threats against our homeland.

SECTION 10:

RESPONSES TO THE THREAT

As detailed up to this point, the Muslim Brotherhood's Movement is well-organized, has doctrine which the MB follows, has a massive infrastructure, their leaders are working inside our system, they are well-funded, and they have support (witting and unwitting) from Americans in leadership positions across our society.

This Movement inside America has been likened to an "Insurgency." If this is accurate, the response in a "Counter-Insurgency" must come from the LOCAL level.

This means local police are the tip of the spear in this entire war.

Local police must work with their city/town/county councils to ensure they understand this threat. Citizens must ensure their local elected officials know this information and allow the police to protect and defend their communities against this hostile threat. This is a long-term effort which must be initiated and worked at the LOCAL level.

Regardless of how we label this threat, it certainly is a large-scale counterintelligence operation that includes agents of espionage inside our government (local, state, federal).

There are, however, tools which can be taken from the information in this handbook that law enforcement, military, and intelligence professionals can immediately incorporate into their daily work.

This section will detail how knowing this information necessarily gives you:

- A factual basis for Reasonable Suspicion and Probable Cause previously unknown to most readers;

- New interview and investigative strategies; a clearer understanding of how to recruit and operate sources;

- Ways to approach a variety of investigations with the ability to see if jihadis are involved.

Analysis

All analysis of a threat must begin with a factual understanding of that threat. The facts must drive the analysis – always. If there is a preconceived notion of what the truth is, and the facts are forced to fit into that notion, the analysis will always produce a faulty intelligence product.

It is a legal fact the organizations discussed in this handbook are Muslim Brotherhood organizations. If that is true, the MB doctrine is the doctrine of all of those organizations. The MB strategy is published and their goals/objectives made clear. This information, based in facts and evidence, must be the starting point for analyzing these organizations.

The Muslim Brotherhood states it does what it does to impose Islamic Law on the world and uses Islamic Law as the basis for its actions. It is a fact that all Islamic law defines "Jihad" as warfare against non-Muslims and is obligatory until the world is subordinated to Islamic Law (Sharia). Islamic Law is the self-defined doctrine of our enemy. It is a fact that all Islamic law requires one-eighth of all zakat (obligatory financial giving) to go to jihad.

All analysis must start with Islamic law as the basis for understanding the Muslim Brotherhood threat or the analysis will always be incorrect.

Therefore, those who adhere to and promote Shariah (Islamic Law) are an identifiable threat to the citizens in your jurisdiction, because Shariah always requires Jihad.

Predictive Analysis

After studying the Muslim Brotherhood doctrine and Shari'ah (Islamic Law), analysts will see the threat in their community with brand new eyes. A truly objective analytical look at the Islamic organizations, leaders, and operations in your area through the lens of Shari'ah will give Fusion Centers and individual analysts the ability to do predictive analysis in ways they thought impossible. Many trained analysts have never been taught to do "predictive analysis" but this is what should be expected from analysts – even on the strictly criminal side.

PRACTICAL EXAMPLE: In the fall of 2010, an analyst who previously worked for the Joint Chiefs of Staff in the J-2 (Intel) section, and who is a recognized expert in Islamic Law, briefed Members of Congress on the coming revolution in the Middle East based on his understanding of Islamic Law, the Muslim Brotherhood doctrine, and the language with which the jihadis communicate. This analyst predicted with specificity, what became known as the "Arab Spring" but was (and is) in actuality the Muslim Brotherhood's revolution in the Middle East and beyond. No other individual or entity – government or non-government - predicted this event. As a matter of fact, the CIA Director testified before Congress they had no visibility on the revolution sweeping across the globe.

Starting Points

Before beginning investigations on Muslim Brotherhood organizations or their leadership, here are a few key points to consider:

1. **The Muslim Brotherhood supports jihad** – what we call "Terrorism." Through public pressure, propaganda, and a widespread subversion campaign, they seek to affect U.S. responses to acts of terrorism and neuter local and state law enforcement agencies when dealing with members of the Muslim community to avoid investigating true threats, while simultaneously prepping the ground for and supporting jihadi operations. [e.g. The 9/11 Commission Report (p. 220) details assistance by the Islamic Center of San Diego (MB front) to a 9/11 hijacker to wire transfer money from overseas].

2. **This is a counterintelligence issue.** Many Muslim Brotherhood leaders in the U.S. came from overseas and learned to survive underground in some of the most hostile areas of the world with intelligence agencies of all kinds pursuing them. Some MB leaders are trained intelligence officers. When they speak with U.S. leaders they have a leg up because they are professionally trained to manipulate others.

3. **Muslim Brothers are not gang-bangers.** Individuals who subscribe to the ideology of the Muslim Brotherhood (Islamic Law / Sharia) do not generally sway in their belief structure and are not prone to emotional tangents. They understand strength, authority, and power. As a law enforcement, military, or intelligence professional, care must be taken when dealing with these individuals to always make clear YOU are the authority figure. When you show "deference" to them to "win them over" it is viewed by them as weakness and submission to what they want you to do. When speaking, do so firmly. Maintain a posture of confidence and strength. **Remember their doctrine obliges them to lie to you.** Individuals in leadership positions will generally do this in a calm and pleasant manner. Others involved in crimes on the street, narcotics trafficking etc, may have a variety of responses.

4. **Avoid working with Muslim Brotherhood entities.** Across the U.S. many law enforcement agencies are unwittingly working with Muslim Brotherhood/Jihadi groups or leaders (CAIR, ISNA, MPAC, MAS) and are unaware of the nefarious nature of these individuals/groups. Local and State law enforcement agencies, Fusion Centers, and others must take an independent look at all the Islamic organizations with which they are working to ensure they are not a part of the Muslim Brotherhood's Movement – especially since the most prominent Islamic organizations in America ARE a part of the Movement.

5. **Identify Muslim Brotherhood entities in your locale, and members of the community supporting them.** Consider interviewing the citizens who appear to be unwittingly supporting the jihadis about their understanding of the true nature of MB organizations. This technique has the positive benefit of educating members of the community about this threat. Members of the community who are knowingly supporting jihadis or their front organizations should be investigated like any other terrorist supporter.

6. **Educate and train the leadership in your department and prosecutors as you go.** It is imperative that police forces at all levels educate prosecutors, judges, and individuals in their own chain of command about the threat of the Muslim Brotherhood's Islamic Movement in the U.S. No state in America is untouched by this.

7. **Never Sacrifice Officer Safety.** Federal agents and officers have reported their bosses have told local Imams about an upcoming raid a couple of hours before or even the night before to "promote good relations with the Muslim community." This example is only outdone by the street agents/officers ordered to conduct arrests without their shoes on in an Islamic Center so as not to offend anyone. Both of these are foolish, dangerous, and unprofessional.

8. **Evaluate Your Agencies Hiring Practices.** With the knowledge contained in this handbook, law enforcement/intelligence/military agencies and organizations should take a hard look at ways the Muslim Brotherhood may try to or may already have penetrated their organization. Most HR departments and recruiting offices for law enforcement and military communities are not trained and are unprepared for this issue. Yet, if the facts are not known/

understood, a police department may unwittingly hire a Muslim Brother or Hamas operative. Evidence exists, and cases have been prosecuted, revealing the MB has and continues to try to get their people hired by local, state and federal law enforcement and intelligence agencies. **REMEMBER:** *This is a counterintelligence and espionage problem first and foremost.*

9. **Prepare for Backlash.** When your agency decides to go forward with an investigation, overt action, or a similar response to something in your community, you must expect a response from the Hamas/Muslim Brotherhood organizations posing as "civil rights" organizations which will publicly challenge your actions. Accusations of bigotry, "Islamaphobia," and similar cries must be met with calm resolve by the leadership of your organization. Stick to the facts of the matter and do not be swayed by loud public outcries. Remember, these organizations (CAIR and others) are Hamas entities and are the threat to your community.

10. **What happens overseas is happening or will happen here.** Cultural norms in other countries that are not accepted or are illegal here in America (e.g. pedophilia, genital mutilation, spousal abuse), are either happening in the U.S. among the similar cultures living here, or will likely happen here. The lessons from overseas can be applied to our local communities. This also applies to violent acts of jihad. If the technique is being used overseas, it will come to the U.S.

Investigative Considerations and Strategies

Adherance to Sharia

As mentioned previously, the Muslim Brotherhood, Al Qaeda, and hundreds of other jihadi groups rely on Sharia (Islamic Law) as their guide on how to fight, and they seek to impose Sharia on everybody else. Thus, they seek to impose foreign law on US citizens.

The first step in knowing if someone is Sharia compliant, one must first understand Sharia. Please see Section 6 of this book on Islamic Law.

Here are a few outward signs an individual may be adherent to Islamic Law

- Wears a beard as proscribed by Islamic Law.

- Beard dyed with henna (i.e. is red in color) in conformance with that of the Prophet Mohammad

- Men's caftan (clothing outfit) is worn above the ankles

- Women wear garments fully covering their body

- Women wear full face coverings with only their eyes showing or women suddenly wearing a hijab (head scarf)

- Men do not allow their women out of their home without a male relative

- Men do not wear gold or silk items

- Men have a piety mark (a large physical mark on the center for their forehead which looks like a bruise)

- Men or women profess to strictly following the Sharia

- Men / Women affiliated with known MB front groups

- Converts to Islam who take on names such as:
  - Sharia
  - Jihad
  - Mujtahid
  - Saif u Islam
  - Mujahadeen
  - Osama

- Parents who name their children using any of the above names

If you observe an individual who has the outward appearance of being Sharia compliant, it is indicative this individual is likely a jihadi or is being "radicalized" to become a jihadi.

Evidence exists to demonstrate that a greater level of adherence to Islamic Law correlates to a greater likelihood of violence being espoused by that individual and their Mosque/Islamic Center (see article entitled "Sharia Adherence Mosque Survey: Correlations Between Sharia Adherence and Violent Dogma in U.S. Mosques", www.mappingsharia.com).

RED FLAG: Significant Change in Adherence to Islamic Law. Most dangerous scenario.

If an individual who is outwardly adherent to Sharia in their dress and their actions, is suddenly observed drinking alcohol or frequenting strip clubs, it is evidence that individual has committed himself to an act of Martyrdom in the immediate future and all efforts to detain this person should be made.

Under Sharia, only a Martyr – one who dies in Jihad – is guaranteed Paradise according to Islamic Law regardless of his past behavior. Therefore, once the jihadi is committed to the Martyrdom operation, no behavior on earth will keep him from Paradise – i.e. strip clubs and other 'Haram' behavior (unlawful under Sharia) will be forgiven of the Martyr.

Material Support for Terrorism

It is a federal crime to "knowingly provide material support or resources to a foreign terrorist organization." [18 U. S. C. §2339B(a)(1)]. In a Supreme Court Ruling on June 21, 2010 (Holder, Attorney General, et al. v. Humanitarian Law Project et al), the Court decided whether non-violent ordinary activities which helped designated terrorist organizations (PKK and LTTE in this case) constitute "Material Support" for terrorism.

In fact, the Court found that if someone washes dishes for, teaches hygiene to, or gives classes on First Aid to a designated terrorist organization, those activities constitute "Material Support." Specifically, the Court wrote in its Opinion:

> "Foreign organizations that engage in terrorist activity are so tainted by their criminal conduct that any contribution to such an organization facilitates that conduct....Moreover, material support meant to promote peaceable, lawful conduct can be diverted to advance terrorism in multiple ways. The record shows that designated foreign terrorist organizations do not maintain organizational fire walls between social, political, and terrorist operations, or financial fire walls between funds raised for humanitarian activities and those used to carry out terrorist attacks. Providing material support in any form would also undermine cooperative international efforts to prevent terrorism and strain the United States' relationships with its allies, including those that are defending themselves against violent insurgencies waged by foreign terrorist groups."

This ruling of what constitutes "Material Support for Terrorism" can be used by law enforcement entities to investigate a wide variety of individuals and entities which knowingly support a terrorist organization in any manner. To date, the Muslim Brotherhood is not yet designated a "Foreign Terrorist Organization" or "FTO," but organizations like CAIR – a Hamas entity – could be aggressively investigated and prosecuted. These investigations will require a knowledge of this threat and courage by law enforcement leaders if these organizations are to be dealt with appropriately.

Reasonable Suspicion / Probable Cause

Now that readers understand the nature of the Muslim Brotherhood's Movement, some of the MB organizations and leaders in America, and the doctrine of Islamic Law, investigators can articulate facts which go towards Reasonable Suspicion and Probable Cause during traffic stops, general encounters with citizens, or to use in affidavits in support of search or arrest warrants.

INVESTIGATIVE EXAMPLE 1: *Traffic Stop.* A patrol officer stops a vehicle for a routine violation such as speeding, and during the encounter with the driver the officer sees brochures from known Muslim Brotherhood groups sitting on the passenger seat, a copy of *Milestones*, or evidence the driver is a member of the Muslim Students Association. The officer now has articulable facts which he/she could use to determine if the driver is a part of the MB or sympathetic and, therefore, hostile. This gives the officer more articulable facts to continue to talk to the driver and lengthen the time of the traffic stop. In many jurisdictions, especially with State Police or Highway Patrols, this tactic will require training of the staff so officers know how to pass the information off to state/local investigators in a manner which does not significantly impede their regular duties.

INVESTIGATIVE EXAMPLE 2: *Financial Investigation / Search Warrants.* An investigator identifies a local organization as a Muslim Brotherhood affiliate collecting Zakat. The investigator knows some of the money collected goes to fund terrorism because he/she has studied "Zakat" in Islamic Law. Depending on the circumstances, the investigator may now have Probable Cause to conduct a search warrant of the organization. At a minimum, the investigator has enough Reasonable Suspicion to open an investigation, gather information and obtain financial records, phone records, and conduct physical surveillances. In some jurisdictions, prosecutors may require overt activity. However, using a statement of facts linking the organization to the Muslim Brotherhood and their hostile doctrine, specifically the use of violence to achieve their goals, will be a good foundation for affidavits. See the exemplar affidavit in the Section 13.

Use Simple Charges to Obtain Warrants

Jihadis/Muslim Brothers need money. If facts exist leading you to believe an individual is involved in jihadi activities, use lesser charges to obtain a search or arrest warrant. In the U.S. and elsewhere, jihadis/MB are involved in criminal activity to include:

- Narcotics
- Insurance fraud
- Housing fraud
- Money laundering
- Passport fraud
- Social Security fraud
- Immigration fraud, etc.

Use these charges to get warrants as dictated by your investigation. For instance, an individual driving on an expired license gives a local/state police officer the opportunity to obtain a search warrant. Once the state warrant is executed and officers are in the residence, if evidence is discovered revealing more nefarious activity, the search can be stopped until a new state or federal warrant can be obtained.

Use Social Media

Jihadis know Jihadis. Use Facebook, PalTalk, YouTube, Twitter and other social media sites to identify friends of jihadis arrested or who conducted an attack anywhere in U.S., the West or even overseas. You will find they have friends in the U.S. and possibly some in your locale.

Identify the Key Jihadi Training Areas

Across the globe, there are a number of known jihadi training areas, schools, etc, many of which are mentioned in news stories when jihadis conduct an operation or are caught prior to the event. Review financial wire transfers from your locale to financial institutions in the vicinity of the training area (for example, subpoena Western Union for all transactions over a period of several years.) Travel records to this specific area from your locale should also be investigated. From this information you can identify jihadis and/or their handler/recruiter in your area.

Interviews / Polygraph Examinations

When conducting interviews, interrogations, or polygraph examinations, it is critical the individual leading (as well as the entire team) be aware of the key elements of Islamic Law which apply, and Muslim Brotherhood ideology, language, and the obligation to lie to protect their Movement.

An interview/interrogation conducted without knowing and understanding this information will necessarily end with questionable results and a flawed analysis of the value of the information provided.

Here are a few tips for conducting an interview:

- Ensure the lead interviewer maintains a posture of authority throughout the interview. Other members of the team may take a softer approach, but if you are interviewing a committed Muslim Brother/jihadist, he will view any lack of forcefulness as weakness and not respect you.

- Read/Study the Al Qaeda Training Manual to see how they are taught to respond to interviews and interrogations. Have a plan to respond.

- When a statement is given by the subject that contradicts Islamic Law/MB Doctrine, state the requirement of Islamic Law and ask the subject why he/she believes it is okay to stray from it. If you know he/she works for a known MB front organization, you know he/she is obliged to lie to you per Islamic Law/MB Doctrine, so keep that in mind throughout the process.

- Ensure the language you use is the language the MB uses. When using words like "terrorist" or "justice" ensure you understand how those words are defined by the MB/Islamic Law [see Section 7].

- An affirmative answer to the question "Have you read and studied *Milestones*?" will give you a solid foundation from which to work. You are talking with an individual who knows what jihad is and likely supports it.

- Do not threaten legal action if you do not have a charge against the subject of the interview.

- Be prepared to be contacted by an attorney representing a subject prior to or after an interview. Research to determine if that attorney is affiliated with/frequently represents Muslim Brotherhood leaders or organizations, as this will drive your response.

Here are a few tips when conducting a polygraph examination:

- Know/Understand the key elements of Islamic Law and how Jihadis/Muslim Brothers use certain terms.

- Do not ask if subject is a "terrorist" or believes "terrorism" is a valid tactic. Questions should be framed in terms of whether the subject is a "Jihadi" or is aware of acts of "Jihad" which are planned.

- Do not ask the subject if he is interested in or supports "suicide" bombing operations. Suicide is not permissible under Islamic Law. However, Martyrdom, or dying in jihad, is. Use the word "martyr" or "martyrdom" to determine if a Muslim seeks to kill himself in jihad.

- Do not ask questions about wives or children unless they directly pertain to the investigation, and do not use these as baseline questions. Culturally, a subject will not want to discuss his wife and may register "deceptive" if you do, even if he wants to be helpful. An honest answer to the question, "How many children do you have?" may not show deception but may contradict information you have about the subject's family. This may be because he will only be counting the number of his male children, because the father views the females as insignificant.

Recruitments

Islamic law specifically forbids Muslims to "spy" on one another. Individuals who subscribe to the MB ideology (Islamic Law/Sharia) will generally not become assets for the "good of the cause." Experience shows that if the threat of a conviction with severe punishment is not on the table, there is a high likelihood the individual will not assist law enforcement/ military in any substantial way.

Even with such threats of prison over them, many will still not assist in productive ways. With this understood, asset handlers should know that even if a recruitment is successful, the handler must know and understand the basic tenets of MB doctrine and Islamic Law or the asset will end up handling the handler.

Natural Allies

If a local or state agency is looking to develop short or long-term assets to assist them, the agency should first begin with members of the community who will be natural allies. Members of communities living in the United States who are persecuted by the Muslim Brotherhood and associated groups overseas, will have knowledge of which neighborhoods, businesses, and, in some cases, individuals are affiliated with the Muslim Brotherhood.

Examples of these might be Lebanese Christians, Egyptian Coptics, members of the Jewish community from Iran, Iraq, and other areas, Ethiopians who fled Ethiopia because of Muslim Brotherhood persecution, and others.

Keep in mind that many of these people will be cooperative, but have a cultural fear of law enforcement in some cases because authorities in their country of origin have histories of repressive and abusive tactics. They will need to be reassured of an officer/investigator's true intention, and that any information provided will be protected to the extent possible.

Females

Law enforcement often ignores females inside the Islamic community as a source of information because police are often instructed that male officers should "never speak to female Muslims." In fact, women inside the Islamic community have proven to be very valuable sources of information and are, in many cases, very aware of the goings on of their communities, even jihadi planning and criminal activity.

Every opportunity to speak with females inside the Muslim community should be made, especially during a call out for a domestic dispute or something of a similar nature in a known Islamic community. Female officers should be present in these circumstances to speak to the female who is in need of assistance.

Officers should simply be aware, as they always are, of other happenings in the household that might indicate further violations of the law. It is unlikely a Muslim wife will speak to police while the husband is in the home, but she may agree to speak with a female officer later. Officers should ensure they leave that door open for a future conversation and follow up on it.

Homicide

When homicide investigators arrive at the home of a Muslim family, it is an opportunity to develop relationships that may be helpful down the road. If the victim is the mother or daughter in the family, and it is not obvious who a potential suspect is, the father or eldest brother should be considered a suspect initially barring any disqualifying information, especially if the father adheres to Shari'ah. If he does, questioning him should be done by someone with an understanding of what this means for the investigation. Writing it off as a "domestic quarrel gone bad" may be grossly off the mark. Sometimes we think the WHY question is not important if the forensic evidence links him to the crime. However, his adherence to Shari'ah and killing his daughter because she dishonored him, should open the eyes of investigators to sons in the house, who are likely jihadis in training. Several honor killings have taken place in the United States between 2002 and 2013.

INVESTIGATIVE EXAMPLE: In the post-incident investigation of the Boston Marathon Bombers, one of the jihadis, Tamerlan Tsarnaev, is believed to be involved in a triple homicide in the Boston area in the fall of 2011. An ABC story stated:

> "The victims were found in a Waltham, Massachusetts apartment. They had their throat slashed, their heads nearly decapitated. Their mutilated bodies were left covered with marijuana. It was a gruesome scene – but also perplexing to law enforcement. While drugs appeared to factor into the motive, the murderer left both the marijuana and thousands of dollars in cash behind in the Waltham apartment...A Waltham investigator...called the murders "the worst bloodbath I have ever seen in a long law enforcement career...There was no forced entry, it was clear that the victims had let the killer in. And their throats were slashed right out of an al Qaeda training video. The drugs and money on the bodies was very strange," the investigator said."

The facts as they are layed out, points to a Muslim Jihadi who knows the deceased as the killer. Understanding how jihadis kill, and how they handle the bodies of those they kill, is critical to handling this kind of crime scene. Similarly, if you find a body with wrists and feet bound with the hands cut off and eyes burned, your subject is most likely a Muslim male jihadi.

Domestic Abuse

Domestic abuse calls are already more unpredictable and potentially dangerous for law enforcement officers than many other call outs. When your agency receives a call for a "Domestic" in a Muslim neighborhood, it is usually a good idea to dispatch 3 officers, one of which should be a female. Once at the residence and it is determined the situation is safe, most officers separate the husband and wife so they can calm down and give details to the officers about what happened. At this point, officers should be alert to what the root cause of the strife is. It may simply be a man and a woman who disagree. But it may not. The female officer should handle the wife and lay the groundwork for having a discussion in a more informal setting when the husband is not around. As noted in the above "Recruitments" section, women are excellent sources of information in the Muslim community. Obviously, safety of the victim and the officers comes first. These ideas are meant to assist you, not hinder your regular duties.

Pedophilia

In some Islamic cultures, as our military and others who have served extensively overseas can attest, having young males around the household who are used sexually by the men in the home, is common. In the United States, this is a violation of the law.

When officers find young males who are non-family members or identified as "cousins" living in the household, further questioning is warranted for the protection of the child. In the event there is nothing nefarious occurring, it does not hurt to ask a few probing questions. If the child is being abused, law enforcement will obviously want to do everything in its power to stop it.

Housing Violations

Muslim Brotherhood Islamic Centers/Mosques/Masjids all subscribe to and seek to impose Islamic Law. In Islamic Law, "Sacred Space" is any territory conquered/claimed for Islam at any time. Once ground is conquered for Islam, it forever belongs to Islam. Areas that are no longer under Islamic control, but once were, can be retaken by force.

When a new Islamic Center/Mosque/Masjid is built, territory is being claimed for Islam, including the surrounding area, up to a three mile radius around the Mosque.

Law enforcement officials and investigators will note that to enforce this, the Muslim Brotherhood, significantly funded by foreign sources such as Saudi Arabia, will fund the purchase of homes around the Islamic Center/ Mosque/Masjid into which Muslims will move. Often times, a Muslim real estate agent will handle the transactions around the Islamic Center/ Mosque/Masjid. Non-Muslims living around the Islamic Center/Mosque/ Masjid are sometimes offered a purchase amount well over the market value to entice them to move and allow Muslims to move into the home.

Law enforcement will observe an ever-increasing amount of Muslim-only neighborhoods around the mosque, indicating a strong adherence to Islamic Law, and that Islamic Center/Mosque/Masjid is likely a Muslim Brotherhood controlled entity. In some states, the way in which transactions are conducted is in violation of Fair Housing practices or other local ordinances, and should be reviewed.

Mosque Cemeteries

Every Islamic Center/Mosque/Masjid has one person assigned who controls the cemetery. If the Islamic Center/Mosque/Masjid is controlled by the Muslim Brotherhood, there will be a cemetery, even if it is not advertised or approved. If a cemetery is being utilized without approval from local authorities, it opens up an investigative door and could end up with criminal charges being filed.

It is also important for investigators to know who is in charge of the Mosque cemetery because if an operation is conducted and a jihadi is killed, the jihadis, if they are able, will take the body to the cemetery for immediate burial in accordance with the Sharia.

Tactical Responses

Tactical Teams must be prepared for a variety of situations related to jihadi attacks. Very few tactical teams are studying the Al Qaeda Training Manual or other specific enemy training material to prepare for terrorist scenarios, and few are prepared for the violence that this enemy brings to the fight.

Often, law enforcement policies, including Deadly Force protocols, will force a team to train to a standard that may get officers hurt when confronting jihadis because they will not be prepared to be as aggressive as they need to be in the situation. The entire chain of command for local and state tactical teams must understand this enemy and the force necessary to deal with it in their hometown.

Here are a few tactical planning considerations for all SWAT / Tactical Teams at all levels when preparing for jihadi attacks:

- Read/Study the Al Qaeda Training Manual, especially sections on reconnaissance of targets, ambushing police, communications, and operational planning
- Read/Study Islamic Law, specifically sections on "Jihad" (*Reliance of the Traveller* recommended, pages 599-608) to understand the requirements for jihad and the enemy mindset

- Maintain a Lessons Learned file from significant attacks inside and outside the United States

- Teach/Train to the lessons learned

- Understand that jihadis do not seize buildings to hold them for a purpose, they do so to make a statement, do as much damage as possible, and expect to die as martyrs. SWAT teams must strongly consider a tactical response as soon as it can be initiated once it is determined the perpetrators are jihadis.

- Historically, this enemy always has observers when they launch an attack. Somewhere someone is watching and likely filming the response. When arriving on scene, attempt to identify likely observation points, and send officers to check those areas out – be prepared for confrontation.

- Look for areas around the site or even around your office buildings that are natural points for intelligence/information gathering. Overseas small huts built outside U.S. bases where water and soda are sold are used as intel collection platforms by our enemy. Here in the U.S. commercial vending stands have been used for the same purpose.

KEY SUMMARY POINTS

- Understanding the Muslim Brotherhood's Movement and their doctrine (Islamic Law) drastically changes the nature of the war in which we are engaged.

- Failure by law enforcement to understand this threat, especially at the local and state levels, puts officers and citizens in grave danger.

- Understanding this information gives investigators and law enforcement officers the ability to identify jihadis in their jurisdictions, end unintentional outreach to hostile organizations, and prevent acts of violence.

SECTION 11:

COMMUNITY ACTION

As members of the law enforcement, intelligence, and military communities, you are also American citizens with a duty to alert your communities to the threat as detailed within this handbook.

The details of this handbook reveal an insurgency exists in America led by the Muslim Brotherhood and other jihadi organizations inside the United States. Because of the depth of their penetration in our society, it is only at the LOCAL level that this threat can be handled. The following suggestions are for all citizens:

1. Learn the information contained in this handbook.

2. Gather and grow a group of citizens who understand the threat and who are willing to speak to others about this.

3. Join a national grassroots organization educating the public on the Muslim Brotherhood's Movement and other national security issues. (e.g. ACT! for America)

4. Identify the Muslim Brotherhood entities in your state and local area.

5. Determine if your town/city/county council members, local police, and community leaders are aware of the implications of the Holy Land Foundation trial – the largest Hamas trial successfully prosecuted in U.S. history – and that Muslim Brotherhood entities are in your state and local area.

6. Encourage community leaders to learn about this threat to their neighborhoods. The initial approach should be made by voicing a concern and giving a few basic facts to demonstrate there is a problem. Do not dump the entire HLF trial document file on their desk. Give them an opportunity to engage in this issue. It is helpful to bring a couple leaders from the community who understand this threat with you (eg VFW Presidents, civic leaders, etc)

7. Speak to University officials about the Muslim Brotherhood organizations (eg the Muslim Students Associations) on their campuses.

8. The most powerful law enforcement officials in America are Sheriffs. Ensure your Sheriff is aware of this threat.

9. Once you have a good understanding of this threat, provide short public presentations on the implications of the HLF trial for your community.

10. Ask your U.S. Congressman and Senators if they are aware of this threat, and inform them of your concern.

11. Identify community leaders, including members of the media, who are working with Muslim Brotherhood front organizations. Give them an opportunity to explain their actions, and use this as an opportunity to educate them. If they strongly resist a factual presentation of the threat, consider other options or avenues of approach. Remember – don't waste an inordinate amount of time trying to convince someone who is incapable or unwilling to absorb the facts. Move on to others in your community who are open to the truth of this threat.

12. Anticipate the Muslim Brotherhood's likely reaction to your actions, and prepare a response. If they respond, it means you are making a difference.

SECTION 12:

SUMMARY OF THE THREAT

The war which we fight is primarily defined *by the enemy* as INFORMATION WARFARE, which manifests itself in our system as political warfare, influence operations, and subversion of our foundational institutions: political, educational, religious, and media.

Yet, our entire government structure is focused on the kinetic war – shootings, bombings, kidnappings and other acts of "terrorism." We are not engaged in the enemy's main focus of effort – Information Warfare.

Where we do attempt to engage in the information battlespace, we are off the mark because we have not learned their doctrine. Jihadi plans for violence here in the U.S., as well as the wars in Iraq, Afghanistan, and elsewhere, are important to the enemy, but secondary to the Information Warfare. Our failure to understand this and to know the enemy doctrine cripples our ability to engage the enemy where he fights his main battle.

Al Qaeda and other violent jihadi groups fight to (1) implement Islamic Law and (2) re-establish the global Islamic state (Caliphate).

The Information War in the West is driven by front groups posing as peaceful Muslim organizations, led by the Muslim Brotherhood (MB).

The MB was created in Egypt in 1928 to (1) implement Islamic Law worldwide and (2) re-establish the Caliphate. Al Qaeda and the MB have the same objectives – the difference in achieving them is timing and tactics.

As a result of documents entered into evidence in the Holy Land Foundation (HLF) trial in Dallas, Texas in 2008 - the largest terrorism-financing / Hamas trial in American history - we know that nearly every major Muslim organization in the United States is controlled by the Muslim Brotherhood (MB) or a derivative thereof.

Documents entered into evidence at the trial demonstrate the MB's presence in the U.S., the level to which they have insinuated themselves into our society, and the ways in which they are achieving their objectives.

Islam defines itself as a "complete way of life" – social, cultural, military, religious, political – all governed by Sharia (Islamic Law). Islamic Law is real law. It is the basis for constitutions in Muslim nations around the world. There is no Islamic Law that does not require jihad as "warfare against non-Muslims" until all the world is claimed for Islam. There has never been any other definition of "Jihad" in Islamic Law.

Under Islamic Law, non-Muslims must ultimately convert or submit to Islam, or be killed.

In Islam. the entire world is divided into the Dar al-Islam (house of Islam) and the Dar al-Harb (house of war), and, therefore, jihad is a permanent state until the Dar al-Harb is eliminated and the entire world is brought under the Dar al-Islam, ruled by Islamic Law.

Current Islamic sources teach Islamic Law is diametrically opposed to the U.S. Constitution. This is not a First Amendment issue, and it is not a "religious" issue. The enemy seeks to impose *foreign law* (Sharia) in the U.S. challenging Article 6 of the U.S. Constitution which states "The Constitution... shall be the supreme law of the land."

MB organizations conduct outreach to the government, law enforcement, media, religious community, and others for one reason - to **subvert** them in order to achieve their objective - implementation of Islamic Law. Current publications of Islamic Law clearly allow for "obligatory lying" to non-Muslims when the objective is obligatory – jihad for example.

When studying this issue, it is critical to read published law written by Muslim authorities, for the benefit of Muslim audiences. In this information war, a principle goal of the Muslim Brotherhood is to keep the West from studying authoritative Islamic Law – their stated doctrine. This doctrine is taught at the first grade level across the Middle East, and in English in U.S. Islamic Schools and Mosques.

Individuals charged with duties in the National Security realm, especially the leadership, who have sworn an oath to the Constitution, must undertake a concerted effort to learn and understand the factual basis of the threat doctrine that includes a self-proclaimed reliance on Islamic Law.

BOILERPLATE AFFIDAVIT

The following is a boilerplate statement of facts for an affidavit for a search warrant of a Muslim Brotherhood Islamic Center. Investigators are encouraged to use this as an aid to their investigation.

A Note of Caution

Getting a search warrant for an Islamic Center controlled by the Muslim Brotherhood based on the below-listed facts should be feasible for law enforcement agencies. However, there is a significant lack of understanding about the MB's hostile intent, infrastructure in the U.S., and their support for jihadi operations. Prior to embarking on this endeavor, investigators are encouraged to spend time educating all of those who will be involved in the process – supervisors, district/US attorneys, magistrates – as to the evidence presented in the US v HLF trial which documents all of the information presented in this boilerplate.

Conducting a search warrant of any Islamic Center will cause blowback for your agency from the Muslim community, especially the hostile organizations which are a part of the Muslim Brotherhood movement. Consider proceeding in stages. First, educate yourself then others. If your agency is working with any individuals or organization tied to the MB Movement, work diligently to persuade your leadership to end these relationships. Through this process, they will gain an understanding of the threat while simultaneously come to trust your judgment. The result will be a greater faith in your efforts when you bring an affidavit forward.

Remember to anticipate likely reactions from the hostile MB organizations and plan to counteract appropriately.

The following Statement of Facts is being submitted in support of a
SEARCH WARRANT for "The Islamic Center of _____" located at
(ADDRESS).

1. The "International Muslim Brotherhood" was created in 1928
   in Egypt with the expressly stated revolutionary purpose of
   establishing a global Islamic State (Caliphate) and implementing
   Islamic Law.

2. The By-Laws of the Muslim Brotherhood state: "The Muslim
   Brotherhood is an international Muslim body which seeks to
   establish Allah's law in the land." (Article 2) It should be noted
   that "Allah's law" refers to Islamic Law or "Sharia."

3. The Muslim Brotherhood uses violence to achieve their objectives: The MB "Creed" states: "Allah is our goal; the Messenger
   is our guide: the Koran is our law; Jihad is our way; and martyrdom in the way of Allah our inspiration."

4. The By-Laws of the Muslim Brotherhood state: "The Islamic nation must be fully prepared to fight the tyrants and the enemies
   of Allah as a prelude to establishing an Islamic State." (Article 3,
   para E)

5. "The Islamic Resistance Movement (Hamas) is one of the wings
   of the Muslim Brotherhood in Palestine." (Hamas Covenant,
   1988). Hamas is the Muslim Brotherhood in Palestine.

6. Hamas is designated as a Foreign Terrorist Organization (FTO)
   by the United States Department of State.

7. A 2004 FBI raid in Annandale, Virginia uncovered the archives
   of the Muslim Brotherhood in North America, including strate-
   gic/operational Brotherhood records, financial documents, photographs, video/audio recordings, and other similar materials.

8. Some of the documents/materials recovered in the 2004 FBI raid
   in Annandale, Virginia were entered into evidence at the US v
   Holy Land Foundation (HLF) trial in the Northern District of
   Texas. This trial was the largest terrorism financing and Hamas
   trial ever successfully prosecuted in U.S. history. In November 2008, HLF and its leadership were convicted of numerous
   terrorism charges including providing financial support to a
   designated Foreign Terrorist Organization (FTO), namely "The
   Islamic Resistance Movement" or "Hamas."

9. Muslim Brotherhood documents, testimony during the trial, and other evidence revealed an ongoing "Islamic Movement" in the United States led by the Muslim Brotherhood, with the explicit objective of overthrowing the U.S. Constitutional Republic and replacing it with an Islamic State under which Sharia (Islamic Law) is the law of the land. (Specifics are found in this Handbook)

10. An audio-cassette tape recovered in the 2004 FBI raid in Virginia contained a speech given in Arabic by a member of the Muslim Brotherhood's Executive council in the United States, Zeid al Noman, speaking to a group of Muslim Brothers in Missouri in 1981. In this discussion, it is revealed that in the United States: (1) the Muslim Brotherhood conducts military operations or "military work" under the listing of "Special work" – this "work" is defined by US Code as "terrorism." (2) the Muslim Brotherhood has an internal security apparatus to protect it from outside dangers including U.S. government entities, and specifically mentions the FBI and CIA and (3) the Muslim Brotherhood has active weapons training camps inside the United States.

11. The Muslim Brotherhood's five phase plan to overthrow the government, entitled "The World Underground Movement Plan," states for Phase 4: "Training on the use of weapons domestically and overseas in anticipation of zero hour. It has noticeable activities in this regard." It should be noted this is an undated document discovered by the FBI in 2004.

12. The current leader (Supreme Guide) of the International Muslim Brotherhood, Mohammed Badie, publicly stated on September 30, 2010: "Today the Muslims...crucially need to understand that the improvement and change that the Nation [Ummah] seeks can only be attained through jihad and sacrifice and by raising a Jihadi generation that pursues death just as the enemies pursue life."

13. The Muslim Brotherhood's strategic document, "An Explanatory Memorandum" described the Muslim Brotherhood's strategy in the United States as follows:

> "The process of settlement is a "Civilization-Jihadist Process" with all the word means. The Ikhwan must understand that their work in America is a kind of grand Jihad in eliminating and destroying the Western civiliza-

tion from within and "sabotaging" its miserable house by their hands and the hands of the believers so that it is eliminated and God's religion is made victorious over all other religions. Without this level of understanding, we are not up to this challenge and have not prepared ourselves for Jihad yet."

14. The last page of "An Explanatory Memorandum" identifies 29 organizations as being part of the Muslim Brotherhood's Islamic Movement in North America, including the North American Islamic Trust (NAIT), the Islamic Society of North America (ISNA), the International Institute for Islamic Thought (IIIT), the Fiqh Council of North America, and the Muslim Students Association (MSA).

15. ISNA and NAIT are listed as "Unindicted Co-conspirators" in the US v HLF case (Attachment A). ISNA and NAIT petitioned the court to have their names removed from the Unindicted Co-conspirator list (Attachment A). On July 10, 2008, the government filed a memorandum to the court which stated, in part:

> "Although the indictment in this case charges the seven named individual defendants and the Holy Land Foundation for Relief and Development, it will be obvious that the defendants were not acting alone. . . . the defendants were operating in concert with a host of individuals and organizations dedicated to sustaining and furthering the Hamas movement. Several of the individuals who hold leading roles in the operation of Hamas are referenced by name in the indictment. A list of unindicted co-conspirators is attached to this trial brief. (Attachment A). The object of the conspiracy was to support Hamas. The support will be shown to have taken several forms, including raising money, propaganda, proselytizing, recruiting, as well as many other types of actions intended to continue to promote and move forward Hamas's agenda of the destruction of the State of Israel and establishment of an Islamic state in its place." (p 5)

> "During the trial, the Court entered into evidence a wide array of testimonial and documentary evidence expressly linking ISNA and NAIT to the HLF and its principals; the Islamic Association for Palestine and its

principals; the Muslim Brotherhood in the United States and its Palestine Committee, headed by HAMAS official Mousa Abu Marzook; and the greater HAMAS-affiliated conspiracy described in the Government's case-in-chief." (p 7)

"The evidence introduced at trial, for example, established that ISNA and NAIT were among those organizations created by the U.S.-Muslim Brotherhood." (p 12) "ISNA and NAIT, in fact, shared more with HLF than just a parent organization. They were intimately connected with the HLF and its assigned task of providing financial support to HAMAS." (p 13)

16. On July 1, 2009, Federal District Judge Jorge Solis ruled on this matter and stated: "The Government has produced ample evidence to establish the associations of CAIR, ISNA, and NAIT, with HLF, the Islamic Association for Palestine ("IAP"), and with Hamas." The Judge ruled to keep the names of these organizations on Attachment A – the Unindicted Co-Conspirator list. A 3-judge appellate panel unanimously concurred.

17. A current edition of the Um Dat al Salik, *"Reliance of the Traveller"* – Islamic Law published in Beltsville, MD – contains a letter of certification signed by the President of the Fiqh Council of North America and the International Institute for Islamic Thought (IIIT) stating this book of Islamic Law is valid and approved by these two Muslim Brotherhood entities. This book defines "Jihad" as: "Warfare against non-Muslims" which is obligatory upon all Muslims until the world is subordinated to Islamic law.

18. The website for the North American Islamic Trust (NAIT) – www.nait.net – states: "The North American Islamic Trust (NAIT) is a waqf, the historical Islamic equivalent of an American trust or endowment, serving Muslims in the United States and their institutions. NAIT facilitates the realization of American Muslims' desire for a virtuous and happy life in a Sharia-compliant way. NAIT is a not-for-profit entity that qualifies as a tax-exempt organization under Section 501(c) (3) of the Internal Revenue Code. NAIT was established in 1973 in Indiana by the Muslim Students Association of U.S. and Canada (MSA), the predecessor of the Islamic Society of North America (ISNA). NAIT supports and provides services to ISNA, MSA, their affiliates, and other

Islamic centers and institutions. The President of ISNA is an ex-officio member of the Board of Trustees of NAIT."

19. The Islamic Center of _____ is owned by the North American Islamic Trust (NAIT). (Insert if applicable)

20. The By-Laws of the Islamic Center of _____ specifically state that upon dissolution of the Center: "All assets shall be returned to the Islamic Society of North America" or "All assets shall become the property of the North American Islamic Trust." (Insert if applicable)

21. Page 10 of the Muslim Brotherhood's "An Explanatory Memorandum" states: "17- Understanding the role and the nature of work of "The Islamic Center" in every city with what achieves the goal of the process of settlement: The center we seek is the one which constitutes the "axis" of our Movement, the "perimeter" of the circle of our work, our "balance center", the "base" for our rise and our "Dar al-Arqam" to educate us, prepare us and supply our battalions in addition to being the "niche" of our prayers."

22. The Muslim Brotherhood's "Implementation Manual" (1991-92) which "implements" their strategy articulated in their "Explanatory Memorandum" states one of the goals of the Executive Office is: "Developing Islamic Centers and supporting them to become fronts for Brotherhood work."

23. The Islamic Center of _____ states on its website it is affiliated with the Islamic Society of North America thus confirming it is a Muslim Brotherhood controlled entity. In that case, based on the Muslim Brotherhood's strategic documents, this Islamic Center serves as the "axis of our Movement" to "prepare us and supply our battalions." (Insert if applicable)

24. [Affiants are encouraged to insert examples from other Federal Affidavits indicating Mosques/Islamic Centers are being used to train jihadis and store weapons – eg Luqman Abdullah case, Detroit. For more information, see websites such as: www.UnderstandingTheThreat.com, www.InvestigativeProject. org, www.ThinBlueLineProject.org]

25. According to the website for the Islamic Center of _____ , Imam XXXX is also the (position) at the (MB organization) OR was educated/trained as an Islamic Legal Scholar at Al Azhar University in Egypt, the most pre-eminent school of Islamic Jurisprudence in the world and the oldest. This indicates he is knowledgeable and authoritatively qualified in Islamic Law, and therefore, knows and must teach the requirements of Islamic Law to wage jihad and implement Islamic Law here in America under penalty of capital punishment for not doing so. (Insert if applicable)

26. The website for the Islamic Center openly states its affiliation with the following Muslim Brotherhood organizations: (List if applicable all known MB orgs associated with the identified Islamic Center).

27. The Islamic Center of _____ accepts "Zakat" payments on its website and states it is "Zakat Eligible." According to Book H "Zakat" in the *Reliance of the Traveller* (authoritative Islamic Law approved by the Muslim Brotherhood in North America), Zakat is mandatory giving which must be divided equally into 8 categories of recipients. Category 7 states 1/8 of the Zakat monies are to be given for the "Cause of Allah" meaning: "Those Fighting for Allah. H8.17. The seventh category is those fighting for Allah, meaning people engaged in Islamic military operations for whom no salary has been allotted in the army roster (but who are volunteers for jihad without renumeration). They are given enough to suffice them for the operation, even if affluent; of weapons, mounts, clothing, and expenses (for the duration of the journey, round trip, and the time they spend there, even if prolonged)."

28. (Affiant is encouraged to add specific source and other information which indicates the identified Islamic Center is working with or controlled by the Muslim Brotherhood and is therefore necessarily hostile to the community).

Your affiant believes that Probable Cause exists that the Islamic Center of _____ is a part of the Muslim Brotherhood's "Islamic Movement" inside the United States whose stated objective is the overthrow of the United States government and the establishment of an Islamic State, including the use of violence in our local area. Your affiant further believes that documents and instrumentalities to further this movement, to include supporting criminal activity may be present inside this location.

APPENDIX A

Recommended Websites

www.UnderstandingtheThreat.com
The author's website. Provides materials and information regarding the threat from Islamic Movement including DVDs, books, training courses and resources

www.ThinBlueLineProject.org
Resources specifically for law enforcement on terrorism and the Muslim Brotherhood

http://www.txnd.uscourts.gov/judges/hlf2.html
Official web site of Federal Court, Northern District of Texas, with ALL trial documents from US v HLF Trial – largest terrorism financing and Hamas trial in U.S. history.

www.GlobalMBReport.com
Publishes updates on Muslim Brotherhood activities around the world

www.Ikhwanweb.com
Muslim Brotherhood's Official Website

www.ShariahtheThreat.org
Details how and why Islamic Law (Shari'ah) is a threat to the United States

www.politicalislam.com
Good source for reference materials and short lectures on Islam.

www.MuslimBrotherhoodinAmerica.com
10 Part Audio PPT Series on the Muslim Brotherhood in America

www.mappingsharia.com
Sharia Adherence Survey: Correlations Between Shari'ah Adherence and Violence in U.S. Mosques

www.InvestigativeProject.org
Chronicles individuals and organizations involved in the Jihadi movement in the U.S.

Recommended Reading

Shariah: The Threat to America, Report of Team B II, Center for Security Policy

Shariah for Non-Muslims, Bill Warner (www.PoliticalIslam.com)

The Reliance of the Traveller, Nuh Ha Mim Keller (Sacred Islamic Law published in USA)

What Islam is All About, Yahya Emerick (Widely used Junior High text for US Islamic Schools)

Milestones, Sayyid Qutb (Operationalizes Islamic Law)

The Quranic Concept of War, S.K. Malik (Official Doctrine for Pakistan)

Methodology of Dawah, Shamim Siddiqi ("How To" Book for MB in America)

To Our Great Detriment: Ignoring What Extremists Say About Jihad (Thesis), Stephen Coughlin

The Art of War, Sun Tzu

The Arab Mind, Rachael Patai

The Al Qaeda Reader, Raymond Ibrahim & Victor David Hanson

Stealth Jihad, Robert Spencer

Secret Weapon, Kevin Freeman (Details Economic Jihad against U.S. by hostile foreign nations)

Muslim Mafia, Dave Gaubatz & Paul Sperry (Details penetration of MB in U.S.)

Infiltration, Paul Sperry

Islam and Terrorism, Mark Gabriel

Death of the Grown Up, Diana West

Message to Garcia, Elbert Hubbard

U.S. Constitution / U.S. Declaration of Independence

Recommended Documentaries

Grand Deception (2013)

The Grand Deception is a 70-minute film by the Investigative Project on Terrorism (IPT), and traces the roots of the Islamic Movement inside the United States. This documentary contains interviews with Muslim Brotherhood leaders and IPT archives of footage of jihadis in America.

Understanding the Threat to America (2012)

An evidence-based unraveling of the Muslim Brotherhood's Movement in America, and how it fits in to the global jihadist movement. Lecture format. 80 mins. Excellent training video for law enforcement, military, and intelligence professionals. (www.UnderstandingTheThreat.com)

The Project (2012)

An explosive film about the Muslim Brotherhood's penetration of the U.S. government. This film walks through the US v Holy Land Foundation trial and the threats the evidence revealed in that trial.

Inside 9/11 (2006)

Inside 9/11 traces the timeline from al Qaeda's earliest origins, through the aftermath of 9/11 and the ongoing investigation, to reveal a clearer picture of the day that redefined our nation.

Terrorists Among Us: Jihad in America (2001)

A detailed look at how jihadis have been in America for years operating among us seemingly unhindered by the communities in which they lived and the law enforcement agencies around them.

Islam – What the West Needs to Know (2007)

Practical academic understanding of the current Islamic Movement, the basics of Islam, and what it means for the West.

Rumors of War III: Target U.S. (2011)

A detailed look at the jihadi threat, especially from the Muslim Brotherhood in the United States.

Homegrown Jihad (2009)

Scattered across the United Sates are 35 Islamic jihadi training compounds known as Muslims of America (MoA). Led by radical Pakistani cleric

Sheikh Mubarak Gilani, Muslims of America has thousands of devoted followers who are being groomed for HOMEGROWN JIHAD. They are called "Soldiers of Allah" and they are trained in explosives, kidnapping, murder, firing weapons, and guerilla warfare. Exclusive video from MoA's own training film.

Obsession: Radical Islam's War Against the West (2005)

A look at the rise of the Islamic Movement in the West and how it confronts Western society.

Radical Islam on the March (2004)

Radical Islam on the March unveils the goal of the Islamic Movement to impose Shari'ah Law on the world.

Third Jihad: Radical Islam's Vision for America (2008)

This film looks at the multifaceted attack on American society by the Islamic Movement.

Islam Rising: Geert Wilders' Warning to the West (2010)

Dutch member of Parliament, Geert Wilders, lives under constant protection because the Islamic world has called for his assassination. Here, this leader of an EU nation speaks out against the threat that faces Europe and America.

The Path to 9/11 (2006)

Film produced by ABC television detailing the events leading to the 9/11 attack on the United States.

Continue Your Education of the Threat!

AVAILABLE TRAINING PROGRAMS

- *"Understanding the Threat" Training Program:* 3-day course covering the Muslim Brotherhood Movement, Shariah, Practical investigative tools for law enforcement/intel analysts, case studies, and discussions on how to proactively address this threat in your jurisdiction.

- *Train the Trainer:* 1 or 2 week program tailored to law enforcement or military units which certifies graduates to teach a course in this subject matter. The 3-day program is a pre-requisite to attend this course.

- *"Understanding the Threat to America" DVD presentation:* Get a group together and watch the DVD, then have John Guandolo skype in for Questions & Responses from the crowd.

- *Tactical Training Course:* Tailored course for tactical teams including combat shooting skills, CQB techniques, and how to respond to a variety of scenarios involving jihadis.

- *VIP Brief:* Tailored 2-4 hour briefings for senior officials of law enforcement, military, and civilian organizations, to include elected officials, detailing the threat and how communities can address this threat.

To inquire about these programs or for more information about the topics in this book, go to:
www.UnderstandingtheThreat.com

Made in the USA
Middletown, DE
18 October 2016